TREASURES OF THE SILVER SCREEN

Remembering
20th Century Movies

Gynnath Ford

Highlands Publishing

Nashville, Tennessee

Published by:
Highlands Publishing
Box 50021
Nashville, TN 37205

Copyright © 2000

ISBN: 0-9676496-3-3

Editor: Gail M. Kearns, GMK Editorial Services, Santa Barbara, California
Cover Design: Robert Howard, Robert Howard Graphic Design, Fort Collins, Colorado
Interior Book Design: Christine Nolt, Cirrus Design, Santa Barbara, California

Printed in the United States of America

To Ruth Overton Ford,
my loving wife and companion

Table of Contents

Acknowledgment

I am very grateful to the various individuals who helped to make this book project a success.

Thanks to my editor, Gail Kearns, for her fine editing skills and suggestions, which brought the manuscript to fruition.

To my mentor, Dan Poynter of Para Publishing, who knows the value of a good team, and steered me in the right direction.

To Robert Howard of Graphic Design for his beautiful cover design.

To Christine Nolt of Cirrus Design for her artistic interior layout.

To Linda Petty, the representative from Vaughan Printing, who supervised this book's printing.

To my daughter, Rebecca Ford, for her support and encouragement.

And to my faithful wife and advisor, Ruth Ford of Ford Enterprises (also my movie companion), to whom I am deeply indebted.

Introduction

Okay, I'll admit it. I'm a movie buff. I have my own opinions. I have an idea of what my favorite movie of all time might be. And I have a list of my 100 most memorable films of the 20th century. They're all here in this book. Some of these movies you may have seen before. Good! These are the ones worth seeing again. Every one of them will fill your heart with joy and gladness.

I grew up with movies. Saturday afternoon double features were a part of my childhood. I rode with Hopalong Cassidy, swung on a vine with Tarzan, solved mysteries with Charlie Chan, and did dumb things with Abbott and Costello. My memories of movies rival sports, traveling to the Rocky Mountains, going to Hawaii, and being with family on holidays.

Movies transport me to other worlds. There's nothing I like more than sitting in a darkened theater and sharing this experience with a crowd of people who laugh at the same joke and shed tears over the same scenes. Perhaps Pauline Kael, the movie critic, said it best: "Good movies make you care, make you believe in possibilities again."

Whether you associate your movie-going experiences with young love, a shared family activity, or with simply feeling less alone on the planet, I hope you enjoy this selection of films. If all else fails, this collection will rid you of "video block" the next time you enter your local video store and find nothing you want to rent in "new releases."

American movies are now close to a hundred years old. This book is my way of remembering 20th century movies and giving thanks to all of the glorious memories they've brought me. May they bring you the same.

Gynnath Ford

An Affair to Remember

Romance 1957

Director: Leo McCarey

Starring: Cary Grant, Deborah Kerr, Richard Denning,
Neva Patterson

● ●

STORY CONCEPT—A man and a woman get acquainted on an ocean voyage and are torn between their mutual attraction and commitments to their fiancés. They agree to wait six months and if they feel the same way they do now, they will reunite atop the Empire State Building.

THEME—The path of true love does not always run smoothly.

FAVORITE SCENE—Nickie Ferrente (Grant) and Terry McKay (Kerr) are met at the dock by their fiancés. Nickie and Terry have no dialogue but their looks and greetings are priceless.

MEMORABLE LINES—Nickie and Terry talk about their future on the last night of the voyage before they dock.

Nickie (referring to her fiancé): Are you in love with him?
Terry: I'm not now. Winter must be cold for those with no warm memories. We've already missed the spring.
Nickie: Yes, it's probably my last chance. We'd be fools to let happiness pass us by. Suppose I take six months to work hard enough and long enough. (He has been a playboy and unaccustomed to work.) I want to be worthy of asking you to marry me.

TAKE NOTE—This film is a remake of the 1939 *Love Affair*. Another remake took place in 1994 as *Love Affair*. It is also a plot device for *Sleepless in Seattle* (1993).

TRIVIA QUIZ—What is the song Nickie first accuses cold and distant Terry of writing? (Answer No. 1)

> *Trouble is a part of your life, and if you don't share it, you don't give the person who loves you enough chance to love you enough.*
> —DINAH SHORE

The African Queen

Adventure/Romance 1951

Director: John Huston

Starring: Humphrey Bogart, Katharine Hepburn, Robert Morley

● ●

STORY CONCEPT—A hard-drinking riverboat captain and a prim missionary spinster motor down a treacherous African river to escape German troops during World War I. Despite their differences and constant quarrels, they eventually discover a few things about themselves from each other.

THEME—People learn to love and appreciate one another more when they have a common goal.

FAVORITE SCENE—Rose Sayers (Hepburn) is transformed when she experiences the thrill of conquering the river rapids. Captain Allnut (Bogart) celebrates the victory by getting drunk, whereupon Rose pours all of his booze in the river.

MEMORABLE LINES—Rose introduces the idea to sabotage a German ship by torpedoing it.

Charlie: We can't do that!
Rose: How do you know? You never tried it.
Charlie: Well, yeah, but I never tried shooting myself in the head neither.

TAKE NOTE—Much of the humor was absent in the original novel and in the film script. It evolved through Bogart's and Hepburn's ad-libbing. Director Huston kept it in. Also, since Huston insisted on realism, the leeches on Bogart were real.

TRIVIA QUIZ—What is the name of Charlie's boat in the movie? (Answer No. 2)

> *Imagination is the highest kite one can fly.* —LAUREN BACALL

> *Behold the turtle. He makes progress only when he sticks his neck out.* —JAMES BRYANT CONANT

Alive

Biography 1993

Director: Frank Marshall

Starring: Ethan Hawke, Vincent Spano

• •

STORY CONCEPT—A true story of the struggles of an Uruguayan rugby team, friends, and relatives who crashed in the Andes Mountains in 1972. Sixteen survived while battling freezing temperatures, starvation, disease, deprivation, exhaustion, and two avalanches.

THEME—Hope drives men to endure the worst life has to offer.

FAVORITE SCENE—After sixty days of waiting, three of the survivors decide to cross the mountains and seek help. Following days of walking, one of them says he is turning back because they're going to die. Nando (Hawke) replies nobly: "If we die, we die walking."

MEMORABLE LINES—After nine days of being stranded, Antonio (Spano) hears over the radio that the search has been called off.

Antonio: I can't tell them.
Nando: Why?
Antonio: It'll kill their hopes.
Nando (to survivors): Good news. They've called off the search. We'll have to get out on our own.

TAKE NOTE—The survivors, mostly 19–26 years of age, debate the ethics of eating the flesh of their companions. Those who are dying offer their flesh, and they make the decision to eat.

TRIVIA QUIZ—What did the survivors burn at night to keep warm? (Answer No. 3)

Where life is more terrible than death, it is the truest valor to dare to live. —ROBERT CODY

The American President

Comedy/Romance 1995

Director: Rob Reiner

Starring: Michael Douglas, Annette Bening, Martin Sheen, Michael J. Fox, Richard Dreyfuss

● ●

STORY CONCEPT—A widowed president, declining in popularity, has an eye for an attractive lobbyist, not realizing that the opposing party and the media would focus on this supposedly private matter.

THEME—The attraction between male and female is strong, even stronger than politics.

FAVORITE SCENE—Andrew Shepherd (Douglas) gets Sydney Ellen Wade's (Bening) number from the FBI and calls her for a date. She has just moved in with her sister and has no phone of her own, so she hangs up. He calls back and she treats it as a prank.

MEMORABLE LINES

Beth: You kissed him? Where?
Sydney: On the mouth.
Beth: No, where in the White House?
Sydney: The Dish Room.
Beth: The Dish Room?
Sydney: The China Room.
Beth: And then what happened?
Sydney: He had to go and attack Libya.
Beth: It's always something.

TAKE NOTE—The U.S. President cannot introduce a bill in Congress (as was done in the movie) even though in reality he might want to.

TRIVIA QUIZ—What does President Shepherd say is not the business of the American people? (Answer No. 4)

> *The man who insists upon seeing with perfect clearness before he decides, never decides.* —HENRI FREDERIC AMIEL

Anatomy of a Murder

Drama 1959

Director: Otto Preminger

Starring: James Stewart, Lee Remick, Ben Gazzara, Arthur O'Connell, George C. Scott, Kathryn Grant Crosby

● ●

STORY CONCEPT—A small-town lawyer is hired to defend an army officer accused of murder. He faces a double challenge, the lack of cooperation from his defendant and a talented big-city prosecutor.

THEME—Suspicion and anger are twins that can get you in double trouble.

FAVORITE SCENE—Claude C. Dancer (Scott), prosecuting attorney, interrogates witness Mary Pilant (Crosby), alleged mistress of the victim, and is shocked to find that she is the victim's daughter. This is a turning point in the trial.

MEMORABLE LINES—Judge Weaver (Welch) to courtroom when a request is made for a dog to appear in court: "A creature that cannot talk would be a welcome relief."

TAKE NOTE—The book by the same name was written by Robert Traver, Justice of Michigan Supreme Court. It was on the best-seller list for 61 consecutive months. Joseph Welch, who plays Judge Weaver, was a famous Boston lawyer who later became a judge.

TRIVIA QUIZ—A two-word phrase was tossed around freely during the defense scenes of Lieutenant Manion (Gazzara). It also got a chuckle in the closing scene. What is it? (Answer No. 5)

> *Suspicion is about the only thing that can feed on itself and grow larger all the while.* —ANONYMOUS
>
> *A beautiful woman lacking discretion and modesty is like a fine gold ring in a pig's snout.* —THE BIBLE

Apollo 13

Biography 1995

Director: Ron Howard

Starring: Tom Hanks, Kathleen Quinlan, Kevin Bacon, Ed Harris, Gary Sinise, Bill Paxton

● ●

STORY CONCEPT—This is a true story of three astronauts taking off for a moon shot in 1970. They receive little publicity and encounter great challenges, including shortage of fuel and having to abort. Houston Mission Control and the astronauts' own ingenuity save their lives.

THEME—Man's insatiable desire to explore the unknown is inherent in his nature.

FAVORITE SCENE—Prior to his flight, Jim Lovell's (Hanks) small son asks him if he knew the men who had been killed in a previous space accident. The answer is "yes."

MEMORABLE LINES—Gene Kranz (Harris), head man at Mission Control in Houston, when told by his staff the space capsule did not have enough power to get back to Earth: "Failure is not an option!"

TAKE NOTE—Director Ron Howard gave members of his family bit parts. His mother plays Jim Lovell's mother, his father a priest, and his brother one of the Houston workers.

TRIVIA QUIZ—What talented person involved in this movie played little Opie on the Andy Griffith program, *Andy of Mayberry*? (Answer No. 6)

> *I have learned to use the word impossible with the greatest caution.* —WERNER VON BRAUN

As Good as It Gets

Comedy 1997

Director: James L. Brooks

Starring: Jack Nicholson, Helen Hunt, Greg Kinnear, Cuba Gooding, Jr., Shirley Knight

STORY CONCEPT—A successful romance novelist is unsuccessful in a life that really counts—relationships. He is obsessive, abusive, and compulsive, but through the influence of his neighbor's little dog and his favorite waitress he takes baby steps toward real life.

THEME—A person all wrapped up in himself is a small package until he learns to include other people in his life.

FAVORITE SCENE—Writer Melvin Udall (Nicholson) takes waitress Carol Connelly (Hunt) out to dinner. She asks for just one compliment and he strains and struggles with this simple request.

MEMORABLE LINES

Melvin: You make me want to be a better man.
Carol: That's maybe the best compliment of my life.
Melvin: Well, maybe I overshot a little, because I was aiming at just enough to keep you from walking out.

TAKE NOTE—Best Actor winner Nicholson dedicated his Oscar to J. T. Walsh, his co-star in *A Few Good Men*, who died shortly before the awards ceremony in 1998.

TRIVIA QUIZ—What is Melvin's big phobia while out walking? (Answer No. 7)

> *An individual dies . . . when instead of taking risks and hurling himself toward being, he cowers within, and takes refuge there.*
>
> —E. M. CIORAN

Back to the Future

Comedy 1985

Director: Robert Zemeckis

Starring: Michael J. Fox, Christopher Lloyd, Lea Thompson, Crispin Glover

STORY CONCEPT—A teen, unhappy with his parents' behavior, gets a chance to go back in time and improve them through a scientist friend's time machine. This proves to be a major task because his teen father has a super-low self-image and his mother who is now his age has a crush on her own son.

THEME—The folly of youth is believing you have more wisdom than your parents.

FAVORITE SCENE—Marty McFly (Fox) hits a bully, and runs for his life. During the chase, he invents a skateboard and ends up being the hero when the bully and his buddies run into a truckload of manure while driving a convertible.

MEMORABLE LINES—Marty's mother, Loraine Baines (Thompson), and his father, George McFly (Glover), meet at the school dance and kiss. Marty's work is done and he is ready to go back to the future.

Loraine: Marty, will we ever see you again?
Marty (with a big grin): I guarantee it!

TAKE NOTE—Steven Spielberg was executive director. Movie has two sequels, *Back to the Future II* and *III*.

TRIVIA QUIZ—The local theater, an adult X-rated theater in 1985, was a regular theater starring what famous person in 1955? (Answer No. 8)

If we open a quarrel between the past and the present, we shall find we have lost the future. —SIR WINSTON CHURCHILL

Bad Day at Black Rock

Drama 1955

Director: John Sturges

Starring: Spencer Tracy, Robert Ryan, Anne Francis,
Dean Jagger, Walter Brennan, Ernest Borgnine,
Lee Marvin, John Ericson

• •

STORY CONCEPT—A one-armed stranger arrives at a small town in the desert to deliver a medal to a war hero, and meets with hostility, suspicion, and even violence. The townspeople have a terrible secret which they do not want to reveal. His investigation leads to justice and paying tribute to the Oriental who saved his life in the war.

THEME Passion for truth has the power to penetrate prejudice.

FAVORITE SCENE—The stranger in town, John J. McCready (Tracy), orders a bowl of chili in the local restaurant. Coley Trimble (Borgnine), a local bully, pours a bottle of ketchup in his chili and attacks him verbally and physically. The one-armed stranger uses judo on the bully, and this makes his companions back away.

MEMORABLE LINES—Rancher Smith (Ryan) to group of men in town: "This man (McCready) is like a carrier of smallpox. Ever since he arrived everybody has the fever and it's spreading."

TAKE NOTE—Spencer Tracy was nominated for Best Actor three times in the 30s and won twice. Nominated three times in the 50s and three times in the 60s. He played the tough guy many times but declined to deliver the eulogy at Humphrey Bogart's funeral for fear he would break down.

TRIVIA QUIZ—How long had it been since the streamliner stopped in Bad Rock? (Answer No. 9)

When you're through changing, you're through.

—BRUCE BARTON

Bang the Drum Slowly

Drama 1973

Director: John Hancock

Starring: Robert DeNiro, Michael Moriarty, Vincent Gardenia

● ●

STORY CONCEPT—A star pitcher and a mediocre catcher of a professional baseball team room together and learn during the off-season that the well-liked, slow-thinking catcher is terminally ill. The heart of the story is their efforts to hide his sickness from the rest of the team, especially the manager.

THEME—A true friend will see you through when you're facing your death.

FAVORITE SCENE—Manager Dutch Schnell (Gardenia), soaking in the clubhouse whirlpool, quizzes pitcher, Henry Wiggen (Moriarty), and catcher Bruce Pearson (DeNiro) about their mysterious activities during the winter months.

MEMORABLE LINES

Bruce Pearson: Everybody'd be nice to you if they knew you were dying.
Henry Wiggen: Everybody knows everybody is dying; that's why people are as good as they are.

TAKE NOTE—*Bang the Drum Slowly* is featured in the video, *Diamonds in the Silver Screen* (1992 TV).

TRIVIA QUIZ—What is the song one of the players in the clubhouse is singing that bothered several of the others, and why? (Answer No. 10)

> *Kindness is the language which the deaf can hear and the blind can see.* —MARK TWAIN

Big

Comedy 1988

Director: Penny Marshall

Starring: Tom Hanks, Elizabeth Perkins, Jared Rushton, Robert Loggia, John Heard

● ●

STORY CONCEPT—A thirteen-year-old boy feels all his problems would be solved if he could be big. His magic dream comes true and he is hired by a toy company where he fits right in, that is, until an attractive executive falls for him.

THEME—Children may believe that grown-ups have more fun until they grow up and learn that adults have challenges, too.

FAVORITE SCENE—Josh Baskins (Hanks) goes wild when he sees all of the toys available in the department store where he works. He meets MacMillan (Loggia), the company president, who joins him in a duet on the giant computerized piano keyboard. They are applauded for their performance by the customers.

MEMORABLE LINES

Susan (Perkins): What were you like when you were younger?
Josh: I wasn't much different.

TAKE NOTE—Tom Hanks learned how a thirteen-year-old would behave by watching each "grown-up" scene with David Moscow (young Josh) playing the part. Hanks then copied Moscow's behavior.

TRIVIA QUIZ—What are the two pieces of music played by Josh and MacMillan on the giant toy piano? (Answer No. 11)

> *Every stage of life has its troubles, and no man is content with his own age.*—SENECA

> *I have lived to thank God that all my prayers have not been answered.* —JEAN INGELOW

Bridge on the River Kwai

Drama 1957

Director: David Lean

Starring: Alec Guiness, William Holden, Sessue Hayakawa, Jack Hawkins, James Donald

• •

STORY CONCEPT—British soldiers and one American in a Japanese prison camp strive to survive. A British colonel stands up for his rights and endures all that a Japanese colonel dishes out. To build morale, British officers volunteer to help the Japanese build a bridge that would aid the Japanese war effort.

THEME—War has the power to cause men to lose sight of their mission and impair their better judgment.

FAVORITE SCENE—Colonel Nicholson (Guiness), after several days in the oven (a box with no windows in the burning sun), negotiates with his captor, Colonel Saito (Hayakawa), and amazingly gains the advantage.

MEMORABLE LINES—Colonel Nicholson continues to appeal to the Geneva Convention's rules of conduct for prisoners of war to Colonel Saito, head of the prison camp. Colonel Saito replies, "Do not speak to me of rules. This is war! This is not a game of cricket!"

TAKE NOTE—The bridge in the movie was built in two months. It was demolished in a matter of seconds and the total cost was 85,000 pounds. The actual bridge in Ceylon took eight months to build with the help of 500 workers and 35 elephants.

TRIVIA QUIZ—What was the appraisal by Major Clipton (Donald) in the last scene in the movie? (Answer No. 12)

> *I sincerely wish war was a pleasanter and easier business than it is, but it does not admit of holidays.* —ABRAHAM LINCOLN

The Caine Mutiny

Drama 1954

Director: Edward Dmytryk

Starring: Humphrey Bogart, Van Johnson, Fred MacMurray, Jose Ferrer, Robert Francis, Tom Tully, May Wynn

● ●

STORY CONCEPT—A young naval officer relieves a U.S. Naval captain of his command and faces court martial for mutiny. Witnesses testify to the captain's instability, but the court martial appears successful until the captain himself takes the stand and displays his paranoia.

THEME—Duty to one's superiors is admirable, but conscience toward what is right, though often unpleasant, takes precedence.

FAVORITE SCENE—Lieutenant Commander Queeg (Bogart) has a meeting of all the officers and explains to them how he knows some strawberries were stolen from the ship's galley. This display of 'majoring in minors' is the turning point that leads to the mutiny, which takes place shortly thereafter during a storm at sea.

MEMORABLE LINES—Queeg (on the witness stand at the court martial): "The strawberries! That's where I had them. They laughed at me and made jokes, but I proved beyond the shadow of a doubt, and with geometric logic, that a duplicate key to the wardroom icebox did exist."

TAKE NOTE—Bogart requested the role of Queeg and accepted less money to get it. Robert Francis, who played young Ensign Willie Keith aboard the ship (his first role), was killed the next year at age twenty-five in an air crash.

TRIVIA QUIZ—What is the name of the ship in the movie? (Answer No. 13)

Courage is the most important of all virtues, because without it we can't practice any other virtues with consistency.

—MAYA ANGELOU

Casablanca

Drama/Romance 1942

Director: Michael Curtiz

Starring: Humphrey Bogart, Ingrid Bergman, Claude Rains,
Paul Henreid, Dooley Wilson

• •

STORY CONCEPT—A callous nightclub owner at a wartime way station has his world turned upside down when his lost love returns with her freedom-fighting husband. The flame of love is ignited again, but there is a greater cause, greater than their personal feelings, which leads to a heart-rending decision.

THEME—Character takes first place over love.

FAVORITE SCENE—Ilsa (Bergman) asks Sam (Wilson), the nightclub piano player, to play "As Time Goes By" for old times sake. Rick (Bogart), the owner, hears the song, rushes over to Sam and loudly reminds him that he was never to play that song again.

MEMORABLE LINES

Victor (Henreid): . . . It is perhaps a strange circumstance that we should be in love with the same woman. The first evening I came to this cafe, I knew there was something between you and Ilsa. I ask only one thing. I want my wife to be safe. I ask you, as a favor, to use the letters to take her away from Casablanca.
Rick: You love her that much?
Victor: Yes, I love her that much.

TAKE NOTE—The budget for this movie was so small they couldn't use a real plane in the background at the airport. A small cardboard cutout gives the illusion that it is real and midgets served as crew preparing plane for the take-off.

TRIVIA QUIZ—All actors in this movie are now dead, but one who was considered for Rick's role is still living at age 88. Who is he? (Answer No. 14)

> *Character may be manifested in the great moments, but is made in the small ones.* —WILLIAM PENN

City Slickers

Comedy 1991

Director: Ron Underwood

Starring: Billy Crystal, Daniel Stern, Bruno Kirby,
Patricia Wettig, Jack Palance

● ●

STORY CONCEPT—Three guys from the city visit a dude ranch for two weeks where they assist in driving a herd of cattle to Colorado. What began as a getaway from responsibility becomes a learning experience to lead them to build greater relationships in their own lives.

THEME—Reflection on the way you live your life is necessary if you want to make changes in your life.

FAVORITE SCENE—Mitch Robbins (Crystal) and Curley (Palance), the ranch foreman, look for stray cows. They find one who is calving, and Mitch gets initiated as a mid-wife. He loses his wristwatch while helping the calf come out of the mother.

MEMORABLE LINES—Mitch speaking to Phil (Stern) and Ed (Kirby):

Mitch: Did you ever reach a point in your life when you said to yourself, "This is the best I'm ever going to look, the best I'm ever going to feel, the best I'm ever going to do, and it ain't that great?"

TAKE NOTE—The crew used a puppet as a calf in the cow birthing scene since several takes were needed. The shot of Norman (the calf) getting to his feet was real footage taken just after birth. Crystal actually assisted in the delivery.

TRIVIA QUIZ—What is the 'one thing' Curley told Mitch was really necessary to life? (Answer No. 15)

A man shares his days with hunger, thirst, and cold, with the good times and the bad, and the first part of being a man is to understand that. —LOUIS L'AMOUR

Coal Miner's Daughter

Biography 1980

Director: Michael Apted

Starring: Sissy Spacek, Tommy Lee Jones, Beverly D'Angelo

● ●

STORY CONCEPT— A true story of the queen of country music. Loretta Lynn (Spacek), a coal miner's daughter, meets Dooley (Jones), an ex-serviceman, and they fall in love. They get married and he promotes her as a country singer despite her fear and reluctance.

THEME—A woman who comes from a poor background can succeed through perseverance and hard work.

FAVORITE SCENE—Dooley wins the bid on Loretta's first pie at the pie supper. He spits the first bite out and finds that Loretta put in salt instead of sugar as an ingredient. He walks her home, gives her her first kiss, and falls into the pig pen in the dark.

MEMORABLE LINES—After their wedding night in a local motel, fourteen-year-old Loretta refuses to go with Dooley into the restaurant next door: "They'll know what we've been doing in there!"

TAKE NOTE—Spacek, who won Best Actress award, did her own singing of Loretta's songs. D'Angelo, who plays Patsy Cline, did her own singing also. Loretta's father is played by Levon Helm, drummer in The Band, his first acting role. Her mother, played by Phyllis Boyen, is in fact the daughter of a coal miner.

TRIVIA QUIZ—What is the name of Loretta Lynn's most popular song? (Answer No. 16)

> *Diamonds are pieces of coal that stick to their job. —Anonymous*
> *Chains do not hold a marriage together. It is threads, hundreds of tiny threads which sew people together through the years. That is what makes a marriage last—more than passion or even sex.*
> —SIMONE SIGNORET

28

Cocoon
Comedy/Science Fiction 1985

Director: Ron Howard

Starring: Don Ameche, Wilford Brimley, Jessica Tandy, Hume Cronyn, Maureen Stapleton, Brian Dennehy, Steve Guttenberg

STORY CONCEPT—Senior citizens find their fountain of youth in a swimming pool next door, not realizing that aliens have returned to earth and relocated some cocoons to this pool. The elderly who swim there feel young again and face a challenge—whether to go back with the friendly aliens and feel young or to stay on earth and grow old.

THEME—People who live in the sunset of life search for a way to keep it from slipping away.

FAVORITE SCENE—Jack (Guttenberg), a small boat captain, finds out his clients are really aliens from outer space. He runs, hides, cries for mercy, and promises anything to keep from being harmed.

MEMORABLE LINES—Joe (Cronyn) to Alma (Tandy), his wife, from whom he has strayed: "It will probably take you an eternity to forgive me. I love you. You're my whole life. I want to go on this trip but if I have to choose six months with you or forever somewhere else—if you're not going to be with me, I'll take the six months!"

TAKE NOTE—*Cocoon* was filmed in a retirement community in St. Petersburg, Florida. Don Ameche, veteran of fifty years in movies, got his first award, for Best Supporting Actor.

TRIVIA QUIZ—What husband and wife (on stage and screen for over fifty years) portray husband and wife in this movie? (Answer No. 17)

We do not count a man's years, until he has nothing else to count.
—RALPH WALDO EMERSON

The Color Purple

Drama 1985

Director: Steven Spielberg

Starring: Whoopi Goldberg, Danny Glover, Margaret Avery, Oprah Winfrey, Laurence Fishburne

● ●

STORY CONCEPT—A young black girl of fourteen is pregnant by her father and then given to an abusive husband who chases away the only person who loves her, her sister. Her self-image is nonexistent until her husband's lover, Shug (Avery), moves in and begins to compliment and encourage her. She flees this slavery and becomes a seamstress who unites with her sister again.

THEME—Injustices either bury you or buoy you; your attitude makes the difference.

FAVORITE SCENE—After becoming a successful businesswoman and homeowner, Celie (Goldberg) gets the biggest surprise of her life when her sister, Nettie (Busia), and her family, come back home after living in Africa. Celie and Nettie embrace in the field of purple flowers where they played when they were children.

MEMORABLE LINES—Shug tells Celie, her new friend and her husband's lover, that she is going to leave. Celie pleads with her not to go.

Celie: He beat me when you are not here.
Shug: Why?
Celie: He beat me for not being you.

TAKE NOTE—Whoopi Goldberg is nominated for Best Actress in her first film.

TRIVIA QUIZ—What popular talk show host made her debut in this movie? (Answer No. 18)

This life be over soon, Heaven last always.

—CELIE TO SOPHIA (WINFREY) *The Color Purple*

Cool Runnings
Comedy 1993

Director: Jon Turteltaub

Starring: John Candy, Leon, Doug E. Doug, Rawle D. Lewis, Malik Yoba

STORY CONCEPT—A young man from Jamaica fails to qualify for the 100-yard sprint due to a stupid accident. He decides to go anyway when he learns that his father has a friend who went to the Olympics and lives in Jamaica now. There is a problem; his friend won gold medals in bobsled. Jamaica has never seen snow and has never seen a bobsled. But that doesn't stop them, and they convince the world that they are serious about winning the Olympics.

THEME—Imagination with determination equals realization.

FAVORITE SCENE—Irwin Flitzer (Candy), the bobsled coach of Jamaica, shows films of bobsledding, which include accidents and danger, to a room full of potential participants. When he turns on the lights after the film, the room is empty—with one exception.

MEMORABLE LINES—Irwin (Candy) explains to Derice (Leon), a track star, why over twenty years before he cheated as a bobsled runner and had his gold medals taken from him. "A gold medal is a wonderful thing. If you're not enough without it, you won't be enough with it."

TAKE NOTE—Based on a true story. John Candy died the next year, at age 44, while making the film, *Wagons East*.

TRIVIA QUIZ—What did the Jamaican Olympic bobsled team name their outdated bobsled? (Answer No. 19)

He turns not back who is bound to a star.
—LEONARDO DA VINCI

All things are possible until they are proved impossible—and even the impossible may only be so as of now. —PEARL S. BUCK

Country

Drama 1984

Director: Richard Pearce

Starring: Jessica Lange, Sam Shepard, Wilford Brimley,
Matt Clark, Levi L. Knebel, Therese Graham

• •

STORY CONCEPT— When the Federal Home Administration
(FHA) forecloses on a family's farm, the father starts drinking while
the mother struggles to hold the family together and unites the
neighbors against the FHA's unfair practices.

THEME—Family traditions are worth fighting for.

FAVORITE SCENE—The auction of all the farm equipment by the
FHA is stopped in its tracks when there are no bids from neighbors
on any of the items—an idea initiated by Jewell Ivy (Lange).

MEMORABLE LINES—Gil Ivy (Shepard), the husband, to his wife,
Jewell: "What if we say things are gonna get better next year. It
never does! . . . I never wanted to be anything but a farmer. That
was my big mistake!"

TAKE NOTE—The film was shot in Waterloo, Iowa. The part of
Carlisle, played by Levi L. Knebel, was cast locally. The boy had
never acted before.

TRIVIA QUIZ—What piece of favorite equipment does Carlisle
purchase for his grandfather, Otis Stewart (Brimley)? (Answer
No. 20)

Hope never abandons you, you abandon it.
—GEORGE WEINBERG

Spring is God's way of saying, 'One more time'.
—ROBERT ORBEN

Dances with Wolves
Adventure/Drama/Western 1990

Director: Kevin Costner

Starring: Kevin Costner, Mary McDonnell, Graham Greene,
Rodney A. Grant, Floyd Red Crow Westerman,
Tantoo Cardinal

● ●

STORY CONCEPT—A Union army lieutenant in a lonely outpost
befriends Sioux Indians, becoming one with them. He hunts with
the tribe, fights with them, and marries one of their women. When
they are driven away, he becomes a nomad with them.

THEME—Life works better when we are in harmony with nature
and we love each other.

FAVORITE SCENE—Communication is difficult between
Lieutenant John J. Dunbar (Costner) and Sioux Kicking Bird
(Greene), but Stands With a Fist (McDonnell), a white woman
captured as a little girl, struggles to remember her English and
serves as an interpreter.

MEMORABLE LINES—Dunbar writes of the Sioux in his journal:
"It seems every day ends with a miracle out here. And whatever God
may be, I thank God for this day. I have never known people more
eager to laugh, devoted to family, and each other."

TAKE NOTE—Beautifully filmed in South Dakota. First western to
win Best Picture in 59 years. Best Director award for Costner in his
directorial debut. In the film, Greene (Kicking Bird) is the adoptive
father of Mary McDonnell (Stands With a Fist). In real life
McDonnell is two months older than Greene.

TRIVIA QUIZ—What is John Dunbar's Sioux name and why?
(Answer No. 21)

> *I prefer to do right and get no thanks rather than to do wrong and
> get no punishment.* —MARCUS CATO

Dave

Comedy 1993

Director: Ivan Reitman

Starring: Kevin Kline, Sigourney Weaver, Frank Langella, Kevin Dunn, Ving Rhames, Charles Grodin, Ben Kingsley

• •

STORY CONCEPT—An unpopular U.S. president has a stroke, and the dishonest chief of staff, who wants to become president himself, keeps it a secret by hiring a presidential impersonator. The impersonator's noble efforts capture both the support of the people and the president's estranged wife when they discover the deception.

THEME—A sense of right and wrong under pressure produces courage.

FAVORITE SCENE—The president's wife (Weaver) and Dave (Kline), the presidential look-alike, leave the White House secretly. They are stopped by the police for a traffic violation. The police officers immediately notice the resemblance to the first lady and the president. The two present themselves as impersonators who had just been to a party and prove it by singing "Tomorrow" together. The officers and the crowd who gather applaud.

MEMORABLE LINES—Murray (Grodin), business friend of Dave's, after examining the national budget: "If I ran my business this way, I would be out of business."

TAKE NOTE—Thirty celebrities, politicians, and newspeople appear as themselves. (Arnold Schwarzenegger, Helen Thomas, Robert Novak, Larry King, and Christopher Dodd are among them.)

TRIVIA QUIZ—Who goes to work for Dave in his new political career when he runs for congressman? (Answer No. 22)

If you don't like the heat, get out of the kitchen.

—HARRY S. TRUMAN

The Defiant Ones
Drama 1958

Director: Stanley Kramer

Starring: Sidney Poitier, Tony Curtis, Theodore Bikel, Lon Chaney, Jr., Cara Williams

● ●

STORY CONCEPT—Two convicts chained together, one black and one white, escape following a prison truck accident. Their dislike for each other takes second place to their desire to elude their captors and find freedom.

THEME—A common goal can lead to fellowship and respect.

FAVORITE SCENE—Joker Jackson (Curtis) and Noah Cullen (Poitier) jump into a deep clay pit to avoid being seen by a fast traveling wagon. The rain and the depth of the pit seem to make it impossible to get out. But one is willing for the other to stand on his shoulders and they escape. Jackson says a reluctant "thank you" for the first time.

MEMORABLE LINES

Searcher: How come they chain a white to a black?
Sheriff: The warden has a sense of humor.
Searcher: Warden said no need to be in a hurry.
Sheriff: Yeah, they'll kill each other before they go five miles.

TAKE NOTE—The movie, director, and actors Poitier, Curtis, Bikel, and Williams were all nominated for awards, but none of them won. Curtis and Poitier's movie careers have now spanned fifty years each.

TRIVIA QUIZ—What kind of tracking dog did the owner keep muzzled? (Answer No. 23)

You can't hold a man down without staying down with him.
> —BOOKER T. WASHINGTON

It is never too late to give up our prejudices.
> —HENRY DAVID THOREAU

The Diary of Anne Frank
Biography/Drama 1959

Director: George Stevens

Starring: Millie Perkins, Shelly Winters, Joseph Schildraut, Diane Baker, Richard Beymer, Lou Jacobi, Ed Wynn

STORY CONCEPT—In Amsterdam, during the Second World War, the Frank family hides from the Germans for two years in an attic over a factory without being discovered. Two other families join them, and Anne, thirteen years old, records the day-by-day activities in her diary.

THEME—Close relationships formed under difficult circumstances reveal and sometimes develop character.

FAVORITE SCENE—Anne (Perkins) and her family celebrate Hanukkah, their Jewish holiday. According to the custom, Anne gives each of the seven a present from her meager possessions.

MEMORABLE LINES—Anne to Peter Van Daan (Beymer): "When I can't stand another moment of being cooped up I just think myself outside. The wonderful thing is, you can have it any way you want it. I took it for granted—the flowers, the trees."

TAKE NOTE—All of the attic scenes of this movie were shot in the same attic that the real Anne Frank and the others stayed in during the war.

TRIVIA QUIZ—While hidden in the attic, what two gifts brought by their hosts fascinated the Frank family and the others? (Answer No. 24)

> *Sharing what you have is more important than what you have.*
> —ALBERT M. WELLS, JR.

> *Only those who will risk going too far can possibly find out how far one can go.*
> —T. S. ELIOT

Doctor Zhivago
Drama/Romance 1965

Director: David Lean

Starring: Omar Sharif, Julie Christie, Geraldine Chaplin, Tom Courtenay, Rod Steiger, Alec Guiness

STORY CONCEPT—A poet and doctor moves easily in aristocratic Russia; the revolution strikes, and he finds himself in poverty. Torn between love for his family and his nurse, his life is a series of ups and downs.

THEME—The casualties of war and revolution are not just dead soldiers, but wounded spirits and crushed dreams.

FAVORITE SCENE—Zhivago (Sharif) returns home from the front and finds his family living in poverty, in one room of the mansion his in-laws owned. To conserve heat, his wife, Tonya (Chaplin), turns off the radiator in the daytime while he is at the hospital, and nearly freezes by doing so.

MEMORABLE LINES—Lara (Christie), his nurse, to Zhivago, after working together on the front for six months. "We've been together for six months. I don't want you to do anything you'd have to lie about to Tonya. Do you, Yuri?"

TAKE NOTE—The breathtaking scenery was filmed in Finland and Spain. If it had been filmed in the Ural Mountains of Russia, the mountains would have been gradually rising peaks, not the dramatic snowcapped peaks visible from the flatlands.

TRIVIA QUIZ—What is the final clue that leads General Zhivago's brother (Guiness) to conclude that an orphaned lady is really Dr. Zhivago and Lara's daughter? (Answer No. 25)

'Tis easier to suppress the first desire than to satisfy all that follows it. —BENJAMIN FRANKLIN

One ought, every day at least, to hear a little song, read a good poem, see a fine picture, and if it were possible, to speak a few reasonable words. —GOETHE

Driving Miss Daisy
Drama 1989

Director: Bruce Beresford

Starring: Jessica Tandy, Morgan Freeman, Dan Aykroyd, Patti LuPone, Esther Rolle

● ●

STORY CONCEPT—A woman comes to grips with the harsh realities of old age and being chauffeured about.

THEME—People can overcome their differences if they'll just open their hearts to each other.

FAVORITE SCENE—Hoke (Freeman) takes Miss Daisy (Tandy) to the graveside of her husband. Here she learns that Hoke cannot read, so she helps him to find the name of a friend on a gravestone by teaching him to spell the name phonetically. This is the first real breakthrough in their strained relationship.

MEMORABLE LINES—Conversation at the nursing home in Miss Daisy's last days:

Daisy: Hoke?
Hoke: Yes'm.
Daisy: You're my best friend.
Hoke: No, go on Miss Daisy.
Daisy: No, really, you are . . . (takes Hoke's hand) You are.
Hoke: Yes'm.

TAKE NOTE—Tandy wins Best Actress Award at eighty. The story takes place over a twenty-five-year period, from 1948 to 1973.

TRIVIA QUIZ—What kind of car did Hoke drive at first? (Answer No. 26)

> It's not how old you are, but how you are old. —ANONYMOUS

> A true friend will see you through, when others see that you're through. —JOHN L. MASON

Elmer Gantry

Drama 1960

Director: Richard Brooks

Starring: Burt Lancaster, Jean Simmons, Arthur Kennedy, Dean Jagger, Shirley Jones, John McIntire

STORY CONCEPT—A sweet-talking salesman joins up with a female tent revivalist, and business picks up until his past catches up with him. The salesman shows signs of conversion but his old habits lead him to new conquests, even the female evangelist.

THEME—Religion and show business make strange bedfellows; one performs for God, the other for man.

FAVORITE SCENE—Sister Sharon Falconer (Simmons) is powerful at encouraging, but weak in meeting criticisms of the press. Elmer Gantry (Lancaster) uses his eloquence and logic to confound the challengers and earns free time on the radio.

MEMORABLE LINES—Gantry motivates Sister Sharon to speak before a group of student hecklers and skeptics: "Big city people have a coat of hard varnish, but underneath they're just as sick and scared as anyone. They're sick and scared to die."

TAKE NOTE—Lancaster won Best Actor award and had a career that spanned 45 years and 78 movies. He was nominated for Best Actor four times.

TRIVIA QUIZ—What famous singer in real life portrayed the choir leader in the tent revivals? (Answer No. 27)

> *The mob doesn't like their gods to be human.* —NEWS REPORTER JIM LEFFERTS (KENNEDY) to Elmer Gantry

A Few Good Men

Drama 1992

Director: Rob Reiner

Starring: Tom Cruise, Demi Moore, Jack Nicholson,
Kevin Bacon, Kiefer Sutherland, Kevin Pollak,
Wolfgang Bodison, J. T. Walsh

• •

STORY CONCEPT—A novice Navy lawyer, who has never tried a case in a courtroom, defends two young Marines accused of murder. Things get shaky as research reveals little that can be used in court, and he considers giving up.

THEME—Tradition is sometimes placed on a pedestal above people, but people have greater value.

FAVORITE SCENE—Lieutenant Commander Galloway (Moore) accuses Lieutenant J. G. Kaffee (Cruise) of being a used car salesman, an ambulance chaser with rank, and a nobody when he considers throwing in the towel and plea bargaining with the prosecution. Her highly unflattering remarks motivate him.

MEMORABLE LINES—The key to finding the truth is in attacking Colonel Jessup (Nicholson) who disciplines men severely.

Jessup: You want answers?
Kaffee: I think I'm entitled.
Jessup: (Louder) You want answers?
Kaffee: (Loud) I want the truth!
Jessup: (Louder) You can't handle the truth!

TAKE NOTE—The play, "A Few Good Men," was the longest running drama on Broadway up to 1991.

TRIVIA QUIZ—What did the two witnesses Kaffee was holding back for the end of the trial have to say? (Answer No. 28)

The man who looks for security, even in the mind, is like a man who would chop off his limbs in order to have artificial ones which would give him no pain or trouble. —HENRY MILLER

Field of Dreams

Drama/Fantasy 1989

Director: Phil Alden Robinson

Starring: Kevin Costner, Amy Madigan, Ray Liotta, James Earl Jones, Burt Lancaster

STORY CONCEPT—A johnny-come-lately farmer with financial difficulties hears a voice saying "build it and he will come." He gets a vision of a baseball field, plows his corn under, builds the baseball diamond, and the dream which changes his life begins.

THEME—Belief in the present produces power for the future.

FAVORITE SCENE—Ray Kinsella (Costner), who builds the field, meets his deceased father, a baseball catcher on the team that appears from the past. They were not close before his father died. Ray asks his dad if there is a heaven. His father affirms that it is the place where dreams come true.

MEMORABLE LINES—Terence Mann (Jones), a famous author whom Ray sought out, gives him a better understanding of what the baseball field and the players from the Chicago Black Sox who come back to play means: "The one constant through all the years, Ray, has been baseball. America has rolled by like an army of steamrollers. It's been erased like a blackboard, rebuilt, and erased again. But baseball has marked the time. This field, this game, is a part of our past, Ray. It reminds us of all that was once good, and that could be good again. Oh, people will come, Ray. People will most definitely come."

TAKE NOTE—This was the last Hollywood film for the great Burt Lancaster.

TRIVIA QUIZ—How did Shoeless Joe Jackson (Liotta) get his nickname? (Answer No. 29)

> *Dreams turn into real stuff. How do you know? Because you drive a dream of yesteryear! You fly in the Wright plane! You visit Edison's lab, and the movie begins!* —GYNNATH FORD

Flight of the Phoenix
Drama/Adventure 1965

Director: Robert Aldridge

Starring: Jimmy Stewart, Richard Attenborough, Hardy Kruger, Peter Finch, George Kennedy, Ian Bannen, Ernest Borgnine, Dan Duryea

● ●

STORY CONCEPT—A cargo plane is forced down by a sandstorm. An aircraft engineer aboard believes a maneuverable plane can be built from the wreckage. Their hopes are dashed when during the restructure they learn he has built only model airplanes.

THEME—Without hope men are only half alive. With hope they dream and think and work.

FAVORITE SCENE—The skeptical pilot, Frank Townes (Stewart), cannot stand the arrogant attitude of Henrich Dorfman (Kruger), the engineer, who thinks he knows all there is about airplanes. Townes, a veteran pilot, hurls high volume criticisms at Dorfmann's ideas, but Dorfmann holds his ground.

MEMORABLE LINES—Townes, speaking of Dorfmann, "The little man with the slide rules and computers will rule the world." (A prophetic line spoken in 1965!)

TAKE NOTE—Near the conclusion of the film, the stunt of taking off was too dangerous, and thus pilot Paul Mantz was asked to merely come in low, run his landing gear along the ground, and then take off again, simulating a take-off. On the second take, Mantz was killed and the plane destroyed. All of the main footage had been shot; therefore, another plane was substituted for the remaining close-ups.

TRIVIA QUIZ—Why did Standish (Duryea) name the plane Phoenix? (Answer No. 30)

> *The person who says it cannot be done should not interrupt the person doing it.* —CHINESE PROVERB

Forrest Gump
Comedy/Drama 1994

Director: Robert Zemeckis

Starring: Tom Hanks, Sally Field, Robin Wright, Gary Sinise, Mykelti Williamson

STORY CONCEPT—Forrest Gump (Hanks), a simple, honest young man of low intelligence and high morals, manages to touch in one way or another every major happening between the '50s and the '80s. He falls in love with Jenny (Wright), his childhood friend, and remains faithful to her, although her choices lead her to distance herself from him in a reckless lifestyle many miles away.

THEME—To retain a trusting childlike spirit is an important ingredient for happiness as one gets older.

FAVORITE SCENE—Forrest receives a letter from Jenny, the love of his life. He drinks in every word, especially the invitation to come and visit with her in her apartment in the city. Her surprise changes his life.

MEMORABLE LINES—Jenny introduces her son to Forrest:

Forrest: What's his name?
Jenny: Forrest. I named him after his daddy.
Forrest: He's got a daddy named Forrest just like me?
Jenny: Forrest, you are his daddy.

TAKE NOTE— The girl in the school bus with the red hair is Tom Hanks' daughter, Elizabeth. Sally Field plays Tom Hanks' mother. In the movie, *Punchline*, Sally plays Tom's love interest.

TRIVIA QUIZ—Who are the presidents Forrest visits in the White House? (Answer No. 31)

> *Simplicity is making the journey of this life with just baggage enough.* —ANONYMOUS

> *It is often surprising to find what heights may be obtained merely by remaining on the level.* —ANONYMOUS

From Here to Eternity
Drama/Romance 1953

Director: Fred Zinnemann

Starring: Burt Lancaster, Deborah Kerr, Montgomery Clift, Donna Reed, Frank Sinatra, Ernest Borgnine

STORY CONCEPT—In 1941, just prior to the attack on Pearl Harbor by the Japanese, an army private, cruelly punished for not boxing on his unit's team, seeks love and acceptance elsewhere. His captain's wife and his second-in-command are falling in love. His best buddy is in the stockade manned by the meanest sergeant in the service. The war begins and their personal loves, hopes, and dreams are crushed.

THEME—The discipline of the military and the independence of a soldier are often at odds with each other.

FAVORITE SCENE—Private Robert E. Lee Prewitt (Clift) plays taps on the bugle after his best friend, Maggio (Sinatra), is brutally killed.

MEMORABLE LINES—In the nightclub where Alma (Reed) works:

Alma: I do mean it when I say I need you. 'Cause I'm lonely you think I'm lying, don't you?
Prewitt: Nobody ever lies about being lonely.

TAKE NOTE—Clift learned to play the bugle for his one bugle scene. Actual battle footage was used in the unforgettable battle scenes.

TRIVIA QUIZ—What actor had to convince the studio he could play a non-singing role? (Answer No. 32)

Facing it—always facing it—that's the way to get through. Face it! —JOSEPH CONRAD

In three words I can sum up everything I've learned about life. It goes on. —ROBERT FROST

The Fugitive
Drama/Adventure 1993

Director: Andrew Davis

Starring: Harrison Ford, Tommy Lee Jones, Jeroen Krabbe, Sela Ward

STORY CONCEPT—A Chicago medical doctor, convicted of killing his wife, escapes and is chased by a tenacious U.S. Marshall. He stays one step ahead of the law as he attempts to solve the murder and prove his innocence.

THEME—Liberty with danger is better than peace with slavery.

FAVORITE SCENE—Dr. Richard Kimble (Ford) works as a janitor at the hospital in order to get some records which could clear his name. He places his own life in jeopardy to save a young man when a nurse asks him to move a patient during an emergency. He looks at the records, examines the boy, changes the records, and takes him to the operating room where the boy's life is saved.

MEMORABLE LINES—After the river is drained where Kimble has jumped:

Official: This guy wouldn't survive the jump from the dam!
Deputy (Jones): Then get a fishing pole and find the fish that got him!

TAKE NOTE—Ford damaged some ligaments in his leg during the filming of the scenes in the woods. He refused to have surgery so that his character would keep the limp. The movie is based on the four-year TV series with the same title.

TRIVIA QUIZ—What is the one distinguishing feature Kimble remembers about the killer with whom he struggled after his wife's death? (Answer No. 33)

> *To be thrown upon one's own resources is to be cast into the very lap of fortune, for our faculties then undergo a development and display an energy of which they were previously unsusceptible.*
>
> —BENJAMIN FRANKLIN

45

Gandhi

Biography 1982

Director: Richard Attenborough

Starring: Ben Kingsley, Rohini Hattangandy, Edward Fox, John Gielgud, Trevor Howard, John Mills, Martin Sheen, Candice Bergen

• •

STORY CONCEPT—A struggling Indian lawyer fights for civil rights, first in South Africa, and then leads non-violent protests against the British in India, the first steps to their freedom.

THEME—A trivial pursuit of freedom involves little sacrifice; a committed pursuit of freedom lays one's life on the sacrificial altar.

FAVORITE SCENE—Gandhi (Kingsley) attempts to persuade his wife (Hattangandy) to clean the latrines. She argues that the job is for the untouchables, and he firmly replies that there are no untouchables in this place.

MEMORABLE LINES

Gandhi: When I despair, I remember that all through history the way of truth and love has always won. There have been tyrants and murderers and for a time they can seem invincible, but in the end they always fail. Think of it. Always!

TAKE NOTE—300,000 extras appeared in the Gandhi funeral. About 200,000 were volunteers and 94,560 were paid a small fee. The movie won Best Picture; Attenborough, Best Director; Kingsley, Best Actor.

TRIVIA QUIZ—What is Gandhi's hobby? (Answer No. 34)

An "eye for an eye" only ends up making the whole world blind.

—GANDHI

If you are a minority of one, the truth is still the truth.

—GANDHI

The Gods Must Be Crazy

Comedy 1980

Director: Jamie Uys

Starring: N!xau, Marius Wevers, Sandra Prinsloo, Louw Verwey

STORY CONCEPT—A bushman in Botswana, Africa, finds a coke bottle and takes it home where it becomes an instrument of trouble; everyone wants it for his own. He takes it far, far away and encounters western civilization in the form of a shy, haphazard biologist and a war-crazy tyrant.

THEME—Man is the only creature endowed with the gift of laughter; the smile is a universal language.

FAVORITE SCENE—The shy biologist, Andrew Steyn (Wevers), is sent to transport the new school teacher, Kate Thompson (Prinsloo), back to the village in his jeep, and they stall in the river. He obtains a motorized winch which he attaches to a tree. The winch not only pulls the jeep out of the water but also up the tree with no immediate way to get it down.

MEMORABLE LINES—The sights and sounds without words take precedence over the spoken word in this movie.

TAKE NOTE—Director Uys searched for three months in the Kakahari Desert to find the perfect bushman (N!xau), who had no contact with modern civilization, to play the leading role. This movie became the biggest foreign box-office hit in history. So they made the sequel, *The Gods Must Be Crazy II*.

TRIVIA QUIZ—What is different about the bushman's speech in his native tongue? (Answer No. 35)

> *He who has learned to laugh at himself shall never cease to be entertained.* —JOHN POWELL

> *The really happy man is the one who can enjoy the scenery on a detour.* —ANONYMOUS

47

The Great Escape
Drama/Adventure 1963

Director: John Sturges

Starring: Steve McQueen, James Garner,
Richard Attenborough, Charles Bronson,
James Coburn, Donald Pleasence, James Donald,
David McCallum

STORY CONCEPT—Seventy-three men escape from a German concentration camp in 1944 due to the efforts of 600 POW's, the largest escape in World War II. Based on a true story.

THEME—The desire for freedom exceeds the desire for survival.

FAVORITE SCENE—Headley (Garner), known as the "Scrounger" because of his ability to get things for the escape, trades food and cigarettes with German guard Verner (Graft). Verner is blackmailed by Headley and inadvertently assists in their escape.

MEMORABLE LINES—Headley talks to Bartlett (Attenborough) about the problem of a blind man, the "Forger" (Pleasence), attempting to escape with the others. "Colin is not a blind man as long as he is with me. And he's going with me!"

TAKE NOTE—Hilts (McQueen) does his own motorcycle riding in the escape. He attempts the 60-foot jump over a fence, but crashes. The jump is successfully performed by Bud Elkins, his friend in real life.

TRIVIA QUIZ—To whom is this movie dedicated? (Answer No. 36)

> *Take my word for it, if you had seen but one day of war, you would pray to Almighty God that you might never see such a thing again.* —THE DUKE OF WELLINGTON

48

The Great Santini
Drama 1980

Director: Lewis John Carlino

Starring: Robert Duvall, Blythe Danner, Michael O'Keefe, Stan Shaw

• •

STORY CONCEPT—A hard-nosed Marine disciplinarian tries to run his family the way he trains Marine pilots. He expects perfection and is very competitive. This creates a challenge, especially with his eighteen-year-old son who is developing his own wings.

THEME—No one measures up when one's yardstick is an inflated view of oneself.

FAVORITE SCENE—Bull Meccham (Duvall) plays a game of one-on one basketball with his son Ben (O'Keefe). Ben beats him and he cries foul; he wants to win at everything. Ben walks away and his dad bounces the ball off his head, challenging him to keep on playing.

MEMORABLE LINES—Ben's father is chewing him out for disobedience when he finds out Ben's best friend, Toomer (Shaw), has been killed.

Father: Why didn't you tell me, Ben?
Ben: Nobody tells you anything, Dad!

TAKE NOTE—The South Carolina home the Meecham family lives in is the same home in the movie, *The Big Chill* (1983) with Glenn Close and Tom Berenger.

TRIVIA QUIZ—What did Toomer, Ben's black friend, say to him in response to Ben's saying, "Your dog is mean."? (Answer No. 37)

> *I count him braver who overcomes his desires than him who conquers his enemies; for the hardest victory is the victory over self.*
> —ARISTOTLE

49

Groundhog Day
Comedy/Romance 1993

Director: Harold Ramis
Starring: Bill Murray, Andie MacDowell, Chris Elliott

● ●

STORY CONCEPT—An obnoxious, self-centered TV weatherman reluctantly accepts the assignment of covering the annual weather report of the groundhog in Punxstawney, Pennsylvania. When Phil (Murray) awakens in that small town the next day, it is the same day. There is no tomorrow. Through this repetition of life for a day he learns how to communicate and change. (If we could bottle this formula we'd make a fortune!)

THEME—Repetition and reflection equals revelation where there is hope.

FAVORITE SCENE—Rita (MacDowell), his producer, tells Phil (Bill Murray) a description of her perfect man while they are eating breakfast. Phil feels real good about qualifying until her list continues to grow.

MEMORABLE LINES—Phil questions two drinking buddies:

Phil: What if there were no tomorrows?
Drinking Buddies: We could do whatever we wanted.
Phil: (thinking of daring options) That's right!

TAKE NOTE—Murray was bitten by the groundhog twice during the filming of this movie. Incidentally, I ignored this film until Jim Hutchinson, a friend of mine who had seen it a dozen times, insisted that I see it. Thanks, Jim.

TRIVIA QUIZ—What is the song Phil hears on awakening morning after morning? (Answer No. 38)

I have been nothing, but there is tomorrow. —LOUIS L'AMOUR

One of these days is none of these days. —H. G. BOHN

High Noon
Western 1952

Director: Fred Zinnemann

Starring: Gary Cooper, Grace Kelly, Lloyd Bridges, Thomas Mitchell, Katy Jurado, Harry Morgan

STORY CONCEPT—A retiring marshal marries a Quaker and learns that a gunman released from prison is coming to seek revenge that same day. He feels honor-bound to stay, but no one will stand with him.

THEME—A sense of duty is stronger than new-found love, but love triumphs.

FAVORITE SCENE—The outlaw and his gang have a shoot-out with Kane (Cooper). One of the gang members draws his gun to shoot Kane in the back when a shot rings out from behind the store. He turns and sees the outlaw on the ground and his wife, Amy (Kelly), with a smoking gun in her hand.

MEMORABLE LINES—Amy to her husband, Marshal Kane: "You're asking me to wait an hour to find out if I'm going to be a wife or a widow?"

TAKE NOTE—The pained expression on Cooper's face throughout the film is realistic, as Cooper had a bleeding ulcer at the time. Cooper gained valuable experience for western movies during his teen years on his father's ranch in Montana.

TRIVIA QUIZ—What former western star and father of a famous actor sang the Best Original Song, "Do Not Forsake Me, O My Darlin"? (Answer No. 39)

A woman is like a tea bag: You never know her strength until you drop her in hot water. —NANCY REAGAN

The worst loneliness is not to be comfortable with yourself.
—MARK TWAIN

Hoosiers

Drama/Sports 1986

Director: David Anspaugh

Starring: Gene Hackman, Barbara Hershey, Dennis Hopper,
Sheb Wooley

STORY CONCEPT—A coach with a spotty past and a town drunk with basketball savvy overcome personal challenges, reluctant townspeople and undisciplined players to contend for the Indiana state championship. Based on a true story.

THEME—People with failing pasts have the chance to enroll in the school of second chances.

FAVORITE SCENE—The new coach, Norman Dale (Hackman), who has offended team supporters and players, faces dismissal at a town meeting in the local church hall. Unexpected support comes from a fellow teacher, Myra Fleener (Hershey), who praises him for not insisting that the best player, Jimmy Chitwood, play basketball again. Other voices oppose him, and his future looks bleak until Jimmy stands and says he wants to play ball again on one condition: keep Coach Dale to run the team. Meeting's over. Play ball!

MEMORABLE LINES—Fleener and Dale debating Jimmy's future:

Fleener: Jimmy is special and I had high hopes he could get a scholarship and get out of this place.
Coach: How about a basketball scholarship?
Fleener: Here a basketball hero is treated like a god. All they do is talk about the glory days.

TAKE NOTE—The boy who plays Shooter's (Hopper) son (David Neidorf) is the only actor on the team. The others are amateurs, and it's difficult to tell the difference.

TRIVIA QUIZ—What were they making on the Fleener farm the day the coach was invited to dinner? (Answer No. 40)

When the fight begins within himself, a man's worth something.

—ROBERT BROWNING

How Green Was My Valley
Drama 1941

Director: John Ford

Starring: Maureen O'Hara, Walter Pidgeon, Donald Crisp, Sara Allgood, Roddy McDowell

STORY CONCEPT—A coal-mining family in Wales raises five sons and one daughter. Work is slow and they have high hopes that their youngest son will find a better life.

THEME—Close-knit families can come unraveled as times change.

FAVORITE SCENE The local minister, Mr. Griffydd (Pidgeon), explains to Angharad Morgan (O'Hara), why he cannot marry her even though he loves her. His excuse is that he cannot subject her to a life of poverty as a minister's wife.

MEMORABLE LINES—Mr. Griffydd and Angharad meeting for the first time in the privacy in her kitchen:

Angharad: I'm the queen of the kitchen!
Griffydd: You can be queen anywhere you want to! (Apologizes for being so outspoken and forward.)

TAKE NOTE—Maureen O'Hara was making movies fifty-five years after this one. She will be eighty this year and looks as lovely as ever.

TRIVIA QUIZ—Why does one of the Morgan sons get a letter from the queen? (Answer No. 41)

> *There are only two lasting things we can leave our children: one is roots; the other is wings.* —JOSEPH GIORDANO

> *I make mistakes, I'll be the second to admit it.* —JEAN KERR

In the Heat of the Night
Drama/Thriller 1967

Director: Norman Jewison

Starring: Rod Steiger, Sidney Poitier, Warren Oates, Lee Grant

• •

STORY CONCEPT—A small town sheriff and a big-city black detective find themselves thrown together by a common goal—to solve a murder. The atmosphere in this Southern town is ripe for fireworks.

THEME—Two men from different worlds find they have more in common than they realize.

FAVORITE SCENE—The time is late night in Sheriff Gillespie's (Steiger) living room. Detective Tibbs (Poitier) and Gillespie, in an atmosphere of privacy let down their guards and reveal that they have something in common: their loneliness. This is when they really get to know one another.

MEMORABLE LINES—At a wealthy landowner's home where Tibbs is questioning him, the landowner slaps him and says: "There was a time when I could have had you shot!" He orders him off his property, and at the car Tibbs gets fighting mad and expresses it openly. Sheriff Gillespie (tongue in cheek): "Why, you're just like the rest of us!"

TAKE NOTE—Twenty years later, this film was made into a TV series starring Carroll O'Connor.

TRIVIA QUIZ—What is unusual about Sheriff Gillespie escorting Virgil Tibbs to the train in the closing scene? (Answer No. 42)

It is easy to give another a 'piece of your mind' but when you are through, you have lost your peace of mind. —ANONYMOUS

A stupid man gives free rein to his anger; a wise man waits and lets it grow cool. —THE BIBLE

Jaws
Thriller 1975

Director: Steven Spielberg

Starring: Roy Scheider, Lorraine Gary, Robert Shaw, Richard Dreyfuss, Murray Hamilton

STORY CONCEPT—A shark attacks swimmers on a New England resort beach, threatening a close-down of the beach and the economic welfare of the village. Three men, a police chief, an oceanographer, and retired navy shark expert, team together to chase the predator.

THEME—Man, at all costs, protects his own from predators.

FAVORITE SCENE—During a nighttime lull in the search for the shark, Sheriff Brody (Scheider) listens to the childish rantings of intoxicated Quint (Shaw) and Hooper (Dreyfuss) as they show and compare their battle scars and trade "war" stories from their pasts.

MEMORABLE LINES—After being slapped and rebuked by a mother whose son was killed by the shark, Police Chief Brody returns home and sits silently at the table with his family where he notices his young son imitating his gestures of despondency.

Father: Kiss me.
Son: Why?
Father: Because we need it.

TAKE NOTE—Peter Benchley, author of the book on which the movie is based, was thrown off the set after objecting to the climax.

TRIVIA QUIZ—What is the phobia Chief Martin has in the movie? (Answer No. 43)

It is hard to fight an enemy who has outposts in your head.
—SALLY KEMPTON

Judgment at Nuremberg
Drama 1961

Director: Stanley Kramer

Starring: Spencer Tracy, Burt Lancaster, Judy Garland, Richard Widmark, Marlene Dietrich, Maximillian Schell, Montgomery Clift, William Shatner

• •

STORY CONCEPT—In 1948, three years after the war, an American court in occupied Germany tries four Nazi judges for war crimes. Justice is served.

THEME—The wheels of justice grind slowly, but they definitely grind.

FAVORITE SCENE—Ernst Janning (Lancaster), accused German judge and author of noted works on the law, speaks at the trial. He is stoic, definite, articulate, and decidedly the most intelligent of the accused. He speaks as one with authority, and eloquently defends his actions during the Second World War, claiming that he was a servant of the state and not acting independently.

MEMORABLE LINES—Janning, condemned judge, invites Judge Dan Haywood (Tracy) to his cell after the trial.

Janning (referring to the atrocities): I did not know it would come to that. You must believe me. A passing phase became a way of life. Haywood: It came to that the first time you sentenced to death a man you knew to be innocent!

TAKE NOTE—Spencer Tracy, at the end of the trial, has one speech which is thirteen minutes and forty-two seconds long.

TRIVIA QUIZ—What famous singer who starred in *The Wizard of Oz* is nominated for Best Supporting Actress in this film? (Answer No. 44)

> *My great concern is not whether God is on our side; my great concern is to be on God's side.* —ABRAHAM LINCOLN

56

The Karate Kid

Drama 1984

Director: John G. Avildsen

Starring: Ralph Macchio, Noriyuki (Pat) Morita, Elisabeth Shue

• •

STORY CONCEPT—A New Jersey teen moves to Los Angeles and encounters karate-trained bullies. He gets some unexpected help from a champion of the underdog, a handyman/martial arts master, who teaches him self-defense.

THEME—Discipline of mind and heart comes before victory.

FAVORITE SCENE—Daniel (Macchio) goes into training under Miyagi (Morita). He suspects Miyagi, who gets him to wax the car, paint the fence, and clean the patio floor, without pay, of deception. Yet, he does the work and is rewarded in major ways.

MEMORABLE LINES—Daniel questions Miyagi about fighting:

Daniel: So, karate's fighting. You train to fight.
Miyagi: That's what you think?
Daniel: No.
Miyagi: Then why train?
Daniel: So I won't have to fight.
Miyagi: Miyagi have hope for you. (laughs)

TAKE NOTE—Pat Morita was Arnold on "Happy Days," a popular TV comedy in the '70s. Morita was nominated for Best Supporting Actor for his role in *The Karate Kid*.

TRIVIA QUIZ—What is Mr. Miyagi's hobby? (Answer No. 46)

I am always ready to learn, but I do not always like to be taught.
—WINSTON CHURCHILL

You are the first, the best, and the only YOU who has ever been created. —TIM HANSEL

57

Kramer vs. Kramer

Drama 1979

Director: Robert Benton

Starring: Dustin Hoffman, Meryl Streep, Jane Alexander, Justin Henry

• •

STORY CONCEPT—A wife walks out on her husband and five-year-old child. The selfish workaholic father must learn to care for his small son, and eighteen months later fights in court to keep custody of him.

THEME—Man often learns the hard way to put his family before his profession.

FAVORITE SCENE—Ted Kramer (Hoffman), having lost his job by caring for his son first, needs a new job in twenty-four hours so that he can appear in court as a working father. The day before Christmas he interrupts a party to get an interview. His credentials are favorable but they want time to consider. He tells them that this is a one-day and one-day-only offer. He is hired on the spot.

MEMORABLE LINES—Billy Kramer (Henry) to his father after the judge has granted custody to the mother (Streep): "You won't be able to kiss me goodnight anymore, will you, Dad?"

TAKE NOTE—The two leads in this movie, Dustin Hoffman and Meryl Streep, have been nominated for awards a total of 17 times: Streep, 10 times, won Best Actress for *The French Lieutenant's Woman* (1981), and Best Supporting Actress for *Kramer vs. Kramer*; Hoffman, 7 times, won Best Actor for *Rain Man* (1998) and *Kramer vs. Kramer*.

TRIVIA QUIZ—How much decrease in salary did Ted Kramer take in order to get a new job immediately? (Answer No. 45)

> *Every man has in himself a continent of undiscovered character. Happy is he who acts the Columbus to his own soul.*
> —SIR JOHN STEVENS

A League of Their Own
Comedy/Drama 1992

Director: Penny Marshall

Starring: Geena Davis, Lori Petty, Rosie O'Donnell, Tom Hanks, Madonna, Megan Cavanaugh, Jon Lovitz, David Strathairn

STORY CONCEPT—Two sisters struggle to help the first women's professional baseball team succeed despite their growing rivalry and the antics of a drunken ex-major leaguer who hires on as coach because he needs the money.

THEME—Women learn teamwork and building of relationships in unfamiliar territory.

FAVORITE SCENE—After the World Series, Dottie (Davis) and her estranged sister, Kit (Petty), the winning pitcher on the opposing team, speak to each other, embrace, and express their love for one another.

MEMORABLE LINES—Coach Dugan (Hanks) and Dottie discuss her quitting baseball:

Dottie: It just got too hard!
Dugan: If it wasn't hard, everybody would do it. The hard is what makes it great.

TAKE NOTE—The All-American Professional Baseball League lasted for eleven years until 1954. It started while the men's teams were away in World War II. Even though the movie has the women playing baseball, they really played softball. (The ball is not all that soft!) All of the actors' cuts and scrapes that are seen in the film were real injuries that they received during filming.

TRIVIA QUIZ—What TV role did Penny Marshall, the director, play years ago, in the story of two roommates in Milwaukee? (Answer No. 47)

In the game of life nothing is less important than the score at half-time. —ANONYMOUS

Lucas

Comedy 1985

Director: David Seltzer

Starring: Corey Haim, Kerri Green, Charlie Sheen,
Winona Ryder

● ●

STORY CONCEPT—A fourteen-year-old with interests in bugs and butterflies falls in love with the new red-headed girl in town, and they become friends. She is attracted to his football hero friend, so he goes out for football. This is a sensitive portrayal of the pains of growing up.

THEME—Young love goes to great heights to gain the pleasure and attention of others.

FAVORITE SCENE—Lucas (Haim), dressed in his best, arrives at Maggie's (Green) home with plans to double-date with Cappie (Sheen) and his steady at a dance. Cappie and his steady had broken up the night before; Maggie is explaining why she cannot go to the dance. She needs to cheer up depressed Cappie by going out for pizza with him.

MEMORABLE LINES—After hearing a lame excuse from Maggie as to why she can't go to the dance, Lucas gets on his bike to leave her house.

Maggie: Where are you going?
Lucas: To the dance.
Maggie: By yourself?
Lucas (in disgust): Yeah, I'm a party animal!

TAKE NOTE—Winona Ryder plays Rina, her first film role.

TRIVIA QUIZ—What is the terrible news, Ben, Lucas' friend, announces to the band at practice? (Answer No. 48)

The magic of first love is our ignorance that it can ever end.

—DISRAELI

The Manchurian Candidate
Thriller 1962

Director: John Frankenheimer

Starring: Frank Sinatra, Laurence Harvey, Angela Lansbury, Janet Leigh, Henry Silva, James Gregory

● ●

STORY CONCEPT—A decorated Korean war hero has been brainwashed to commit pending political assassinations. His war buddies could prevent this if they could only remember what happened. A classic suspense thriller.

THEME—The mind of man is complex and more susceptible to suggestions, good or evil, during times of extreme stress.

FAVORITE SCENE—Raymond Shaw (Harvey), decorated war hero, agonizes as he bares his heart to his friend and former prisoner-of-war, Marco (Sinatra), about his hatred for his mother (Lansbury), who broke up his courtship with his one true love.

MEMORABLE LINES—Dr. Yen Lo (Khigh Dhiegh), the Chinese communist in charge of prisoners-of-war, refers to his chief guinea pig, Raymond Shaw, with these words: "His brain has not only been washed, as they say, it's been dry-cleaned!"

TAKE NOTE—Lansbury, nominated for Best Supporting Actress, was thirty-seven when she played the role of Harvey's mother. He was thirty-four. There were no doubles in the fight scene between Frank Sinatra and Henry Silva where Frank broke his finger.

TRIVIA QUIZ—This was the favorite film of what president? (Answer No. 49)

> *When a man does not know what harbor he is making for, no wind is right.* —LATIN PROVERB

> *A man has no more character than he can command in a time of crisis.* —RALPH W. SOCKMAN

The Man in the Moon

Drama 1991

Director: Robert Mulligan

Starring: Reese Witherspoon, Emily Warfield, Sam Waterston, Tess Harper, Jason Landon, Gail Strickland

STORY CONCEPT—Two devoted sisters, ages fourteen and seventeen, go their separate ways when they both fall in love with the seventeen-year-old boy next door. He prefers the older sister. It isn't until a crisis occurs that the two sisters come together again with renewed love.

THEME—Sibling rivalry changes to sibling support when the need arises.

FAVORITE SCENE—Fourteen-year-old Dani (Witherspoon), infatuated with Curt (London), agrees to meet him at night at a swimming hole. A storm comes up and Dani's pregnant mother (Harper) finds her missing. While searching for her, she injures herself and is taken to the hospital.

MEMORABLE LINES—Abigail and Matthew Trant (Waterston), concerned parents, talk about Dani and her exploits.

Matthew: She is too big to be out wandering about.
Abigail: How come she's too big? She used to be too little! She must have passed "just right" when you weren't looking!

TAKE NOTE—The director, Robert Mulligan, directed *To Kill a Mockingbird* twenty-nine years before he directed this winning film.

TRIVIA QUIZ—How did Maureen (Warfield) teach her younger sister, Dani, to practice for her first kiss? (Answer No. 50)

> *Think of all the beauty still left around you and be happy.*
> —ANNE FRANK

> *The only thing I ever said to my parents when I was a teenager was, 'Hang up, I got it.'* —CAROL LEIFER

The Man Who Knew Too Much
Thriller 1956

Director: Alfred Hitchcock

Starring: Jimmy Stewart, Doris Day, Christopher Olsen

STORY CONCEPT—An American boy is kidnapped in French Morocco because his parents may know something about an assassination. A medical doctor and his wife, a famous singer, begin the journey in search of their son and it leads to London.

THEME—A little knowledge can be a dangerous thing.

FAVORITE SCENE—Dr. Ben McKenna (Stewart) prepares his wife for the bad news that their son has been kidnapped, by insisting that she take a sedative beforehand. She resists but he persuades her to do so. The sedative is beginning to take effect when he drops the bombshell on her. For a minute or two she is out of control but the medication does its job.

MEMORABLE LINES—Jo (Day), Dr. McKenna's wife, has been asked to sing at the Moroccan embassy where their son, Hank (Olsen), is held captive. She sings the song "Que, Sera, Sera" so loudly that Hank hears her and recognizes her voice.

Hank: That's my mother's voice!

Mrs. Drayton (the lady who is guarding Hank and is determined to see him escape): Can you whistle that song? Whistle it as loud as you can! (Hank's father hears the whistle and comes to the rescue.)

TAKE NOTE—The Royal Albert Hall sequence near the end of the film when the London Symphony is performing lasts twelve minutes without a single word of dialogue.

TRIVIA QUIZ—What nervous habit does Dr. McKenna display when Mr. Drayton is phoning the hotel from the police station? (Answer No. 51)

> *He who deliberates fully before taking a step will spend his entire life on one leg.* —CHINESE PROVERB

The Man Who Shot Liberty Valance
Western 1962

Director: John Ford

Starring: John Wayne, Jimmy Stewart, Vera Miles, Edmond O'Brien, Lee Marvin, Woody Strode, Andy Devine, Strother Martin

STORY CONCEPT—A lawyer in the old west, now a senator, who became famous for killing a notorious outlaw, returns to Shinbone when he learns of his friend's death. He now tells the truth about what really happened years ago.

THEME—A self-made man is a myth; many people have touched our lives and we are a composite of all of them.

FAVORITE SCENE—Mr. Peabody (O'Brien), editor of the Shinbone Star, presides at the nomination of delegates to the first convention for statehood. Outlaws, led by Liberty Valance (Marvin), attempt to take over but fail. A new lawyer in town, Ransom Stoddard (Stewart), is selected to go.

MEMORABLE LINES—Senator Stoddard complains about the burial arrangements for his friend, Tom Donevant (Wayne), when he comes back to Shinbone from the capitol. The local undertaker says: "The county is going to bury him, you know. I'm not going to make a nickel out of it."

TAKE NOTE—Jimmy Stewart starred in seventeen westerns, John Wayne in thirty-six. Both starred in Wayne's last movie, *The Shootist*, the story of a dying gunfighter.

TRIVIA QUIZ—What was the flower that held such significance for Hallie Stoddard (Miles), the woman both Ransom and Tom loved? (Answer No. 52)

> *When a friend is in trouble, don't annoy him by asking if there is anything you can do. Think up something appropriate and do it.*
> —EDGAR WATSON HOWE

Moonstruck

Comedy/Romance 1987

Director: Norman Jewison

Starring: Cher, Nicolas Cage, Danny Aiello, Vincent Gardenia,
Olympia Dukakis

STORY CONCEPT—A spirited widow, weary of waiting, is about to remarry when she falls in love with her fiancé's younger brother.

THEME—The three R's in the school of love are recognition, reassurance, and romance.

FAVORITE SCENE—Breakfast time in the Castorini home is wake-up time when Loretta (Cher) introduces her new love, Ronny (Cage), and her mother, Rose (Dukakis) demands that her husband's (Gardenia's) love affair stop at once. Mr. Castorini stands up, glares at her, bangs on the table, and sits down without saying a word. Loretta's fiancé, Johnny (Aiello), comes in, having just returned from Sicily where his mother is dying. He has good news and bad news. The good news is that his mother has had a miraculous recovery. The bad new is that he cannot marry Loretta. This seems to solve her problem.

MEMORABLE LINES—Loretta hangs up the phone after talking with Johnny, her fiancé, who is in Sicily at the bedside of his dying mother.

Rose: How's the mother?
Loretta: She's dying, but I could still hear her big mouth!

TAKE NOTE—Nicolas Cage plays Ronny, a man with only one hand. In Cage's previous role in *Peggy Sue Got Married* (1986), Cage's character begged Peggy Sue to marry him, saying he doesn't know what the future holds; he might lose his hand.

TRIVIA QUIZ—What verse of song sung by Dean Martin explains the title of this movie? (Answer No. 54)

Spring is God's way of saying, 'One more time!'

—ROBERT ORBEN

Mr. Holland's Opus

Drama 1995

Director: Stephen Herek

Starring: Richard Dreyfuss, Glenne Headly, Jay Thomas, Olympia Dukakis, Anthony Natale

STORY CONCEPT—A frustrated composer finds fulfillment as a high school music teacher. The effect he has on children whom he teaches is invaluable.

THEME—A detour in life often leads one to find true values.

FAVORITE SCENE—At a school concert Mr. Holland (Dreyfuss) dedicates the song "Beautiful Boy" to his hearing impaired son, Cole (Natale), and then sings and communicates it in sign language for him. This is the turning point in their strained relationship.

MEMORABLE LINES—Holland is sixty years of age and finds that his services are no longer needed due to a lack of funding. His response: "The day they cut the football budget in this state, that will be the end of Western Civilization as we know it!"

TAKE NOTE—Dreyfuss, nominated for Best Actor, has worked in movies for thirty-three years. He won Best Actor award in 1977 for *The Goodbye Girl*.

TRIVIA QUIZ—Who wrote the song "Beautiful Boy"? (Answer No. 53)

> *The teacher is like the candle, which lights others in consuming itself.* —ITALIAN PROVERB
>
> *Life is what happens to you when you're planning something else.*
> —ANONYMOUS

Mrs. Miniver

Drama/War 1942

Director: William Wyler

Starring: Greer Garson, Walter Pidgeon, Dame Mae Whitty, Teresa Wright, Richard Ney

● ●

STORY CONCEPT—The Miniver family survives bombings, shortages, loneliness, and even death of loved ones in the beginning stages of the Second World War in Great Britain.

THEME—The limits to which the human spirit can endure are forever to be explored.

FAVORITE SCENE—In the midst of all the chaos, the local village flower show is held; Lady Beldon (Whitty) has won the first prize for the best rose every year. Will she continue her winning streak?

MEMORABLE LINES—The Vicar (minister), standing in a shell of a church, speaks to his congregation and to empty pews where children and old people—victims of the war—once sat. He asks and answers the question: "Why should they be sacrificed? Because this is not only a war of soldiers in uniform but of the people, all the people. It must be fought not only on the battlefield, but in the factories, in the homes, and in the heart." (This speech was so moving that President Roosevelt had it printed in leaflets and air-dropped over occupied Europe.)

TAKE NOTE—Winston Churchill announced that *Mrs. Miniver*, the movie, was more valuable in England than the combined efforts of six divisions!

TRIVIA QUIZ—In their bomb shelter, Mrs. Miniver (Garson) is reading a book to her children, the first book Mr. Miniver (Pidgeon) and Mrs. Miniver had read when they were both children. What is the name of the book? (Answer No. 55)

No one is fool enough to choose war instead of peace. For in peace sons bury fathers, but in war fathers bury sons. —HERODOTUS

Murphy's Romance
Comedy/Romance 1985

Director: Martin Ritt

Starring: Sally Field, James Garner, Corey Haim, Brian Kerwin

STORY CONCEPT—A young divorcée moves to a farm in Arizona with her twelve-year-old son where she meets an older laid-back widowed pharmacist who is helpful in getting her son a job and money for her to run her ranch. He becomes her friend, a very close friend, and things go well until her ex-husband shows up and becomes a rival for her affections.

THEME—A feeling of safety and dependability are necessary ingredients for a harmonious relationship between couples.

FAVORITE SCENE—Emma Moriarty (Field) is hospitalized after a minor auto accident. Murphy Jones (Garner), the pharmacist, visits her, listens to her tale of woe, watches her cry—then tells her some good news that makes her smile. Her financial difficulties are alleviated.

MEMORABLE LINES—Moriarty (Field) applies for a bank loan:

Loan Officer: What security do you have?
Moriarty: Me.
Loan Officer: If you were only a man . . .
Moriarty: You mean if I had a fly instead of a zipper I'd get a loan!
(She storms out mad.)

TAKE NOTE—After thirty years in the movies, James Garner is nominated for his first Oscar—Best Supporting Actor. Young Jake (Haim) plays the lead in *Lucas*, another selection in this book.

TRIVIA QUIZ—What model mint-condition automobile does Murphy keep parked in front of his business? (Answer No. 56)

Opportunity is missed by most people because it is dressed in overalls and looks like work. —THOMAS EDISON

68

The Music Man

Musical/Romance 1962

Director: Morton DaCosta

Starring: Robert Preston, Shirley Jones, Buddy Hackett, Hermione Gingold, Paul Ford, Ron Howard

STORY CONCEPT—A con man professor (Preston) posing as a band director comes to River City, Iowa, to get the town's money by recruiting young people to join the band and buy instruments which he would never deliver. He is very persuasive and his plan works until he meets a lovely lady who challenges him to change.

THEME—Some love money and use people; others love people and use money. The latter is the kind that endures.

FAVORITE SCENE—Professor Hill reveals to Winthrop (Howard) that he is a fake and a liar while Marion (Jones) listens to his confession.

MEMORABLE LINES—Professor Hill asks Marion to go out with him.

Marion: Maybe, tomorrow.
Hill: You pile up a lot of tomorrows, you'll find you're left with nothing but a lot of empty yesterdays. I don't know about you but I'd like to make today worth remembering!

TAKE NOTE—*The Music Man* is a musical by Meredith Wilson and Frank Lacey, which first appeared on stage with Robert Preston playing the lead role of "Professor." River City is based on Wilson's home town of Mason City, Iowa.

TRIVIA QUIZ—How many trombones are being played in the closing scene? (Answer No. 57)

Some people are more concerned about 'deals' than ideals.

—ANONYMOUS

My Life

Drama 1993

Director: Bruce Joel Rubin

Starring: Michael Keaton, Nicole Kidman, Haing S. Ngor, Queen Latifah

STORY CONCEPT—An upwardly mobile businessman has lung cancer and is expected to die before his wife gives birth to their first child. He prepares self-video tapes for his son to view. He seeks alternative healing treatments which motivate him to work on healing communication breakdowns between himself, his wife, and his parents.

THEME—To get a glimpse of the end can be a new beginning.

FAVORITE SCENE—Bob Jones (Keaton) is a basket case as he brings his video camera to the delivery room. He needs more care than his wife, as her new son is delivered.

MEMORABLE LINES—Bob finds out more about himself as he listens to Mr. Ho (Ngor), an alternative healing specialist.

Mr. Ho: Why did you marry your wife?
Bob: She was a very good person.
Mr. Ho: It is not enough to marry goodness. You have to find it in yourself.

TAKE NOTE—Michael Keaton and Nicole Kidman who play husband and wife in this movie have something else in common. He played Batman in *Batman Returns* (1992) and she played a psychologist in *Batman Forever* (1995).

TRIVIA QUIZ—When Bob visits the home of his youth in Detroit, what does he find in a secret place behind a cornerstone? (Answer No. 58)

Life is not lost by dying; life is lost minute by minute, day by day, in all the thousand small, uncaring ways.

—STEPHEN SAINT VINCENT BENET

North by Northwest
Thriller/Drama 1959

Director: Alfred Hitchcock

Starring: Cary Grant, Eva Marie Saint, James Mason,
Leo G. Carroll, Martin Landau, Jessie Royce Landis

● ●

STORY CONCEPT—An advertising executive is mistaken for a government agent and is chased across the country by both spies and the law.

THEME—The desire for survival motivates a man to take chances beyond what he normally would take.

FAVORITE SCENE—Roger Thornhill (Grant) finds himself in the midwest plains after stepping off the bus at an isolated location. A crop-dusting plane appears and shots ring out. Roger, realizing his life is in jeopardy and that the plane is to "dust him off," runs for his life. He drops to the ground and looks up to see the plane crashing into a fuel tanker truck driving down the highway.

MEMORABLE LINES—Roger and an attractive lady strike up a conversation after meeting in the dining car of a train. Eve Kendall (Saint) shows an above-average interest in him.

Eve: My problem is I'm always meeting men who don't believe in marriage.
Roger: Not me. I've been married twice!
Eve: See what I mean!

TAKE NOTE—Director Hitchcock wanted Grant to have a sneezing fit on the nose of Lincoln (Mt. Rushmore), but the U.S. government would not permit it. They didn't want anyone playing around with such a sacred monument, much less Lincoln's nose.

TRIVIA QUIZ—What is the one thing Alfred Hitchcock does in all of his movies? (Answer No. 59)

> *But screw your courage to the sticking place and we'll not fail.*
> —WILLIAM SHAKESPEARE

Notorious

Thriller/Romance 1946

Director: Alfred Hitchcock

Starring: Cary Grant, Ingrid Bergman, Claude Raines, Louis Calhern

• •

STORY CONCEPT—An American government agent influences the daughter of a disgraced father to infiltrate a post-World War II spy ring in Brazil. He puts her life in jeopardy, although he has grown to love her.

THEME—All is fair in love and espionage.

FAVORITE SCENE—Devlin (Grant) needs the key to the wine cellar where secrets are stored. According to his instructions the key is stolen by Alicia (Bergman) from her husband Sebastian (Rains) whom she has married to get the information on the spy ring. She is almost found out by her husband but manages to pass the key on to Devlin and the secret is discovered.

MEMORABLE LINES—During a romantic interlude between Alicia and Devlin:

Alicia: This is a strange love affair.
Devlin: What's strange about it?
Alicia: The fact that you don't love me.

TAKE NOTE—Roger Ebert, popular film critic, put this movie on his top ten list of all time in 1982.

TRIVIA QUIZ—In what scene in this movie do you see the cameo by director Hitchcock? (Answer No. 60)

Jests that give pain are no jests. —CERVANTES

Living a double life will get you nowhere twice as fast.

—JOHN MASON

October Sky
Biography/Drama 1999

Director: Joe Johnston

Starring: Jake Gyllenhaal, Chris Cooper, Laura Dern

● ●

STORY CONCEPT—In 1957, Homer Hickam, a high school student in a coal mining community in West Virginia, sets out to build a rocket despite the strong disapproval of his father and the jeers of his peers. Only two miners and a school teacher cheer him on.

THEME—A dream is not what you see in your surroundings but what you see in your mind.

FAVORITE SCENE—Homer (Gyllenhaal) returns home from the science fair and visits his father (Cooper), a supervisor at the mine. When Homer's project was stolen at the science fair his dad was responsible for getting the spare parts. This classic hardened father shows his soft side when Homer looks into his dust-caked face and says "thank you." This is the beginning of a better relationship between father and son.

MEMORABLE LINES—Ms. Riley (Dern) has Hodgkins disease and is in the hospital. Homer shows her the medal he won for his rocket project at the science fair.

Ms. Riley: I'm so proud to be your teacher. Can I hold the medal?
Homer: It's yours. We wouldn't have won it without you. (He pins it to her pillow.)

TAKE NOTE—Homer Hickam, the successful rocket builder, became a trainer of astronauts for NASA in later years.

TRIVIA QUIZ—What motivated Homer to want to build a rocket? (Answer No. 61)

> *If you would hit the mark, you must aim a little above it; every arrow that flies feels the attraction of earth.*
> —HENRY WADSWORTH LONGFELLOW

On the Waterfront

Drama 1954

Director: Elia Kazan

Starring: Marlon Brando, Eva Marie Saint, Karl Malden, Rod Steiger, Lee J. Cobb

STORY CONCEPT—Corruption and murder by union leaders on the waterfront cause an outcry by a courageous priest who motivates a former prize fighter, brother to one of the leaders, to take the high road and end the corruption.

THEME—Corruption and crime are strong but these forces underestimate the power of a human spirit with conscience.

FAVORITE SCENE—Terry Malloy (Brando), a former prize fighter, and Edie Doyle (Saint), whose brother was killed by the mob, debate their two philosophies of life at a restaurant on their first date. Her belief: Everyone should care for and help everybody else. His belief: Do it to others before they do it to you.

MEMORABLE LINES—Father Barry (Malden) encourages Terry to follow his conscience and testify before the congressional hearing about crime on the waterfront.

Terry: Conscience, that's something that'll drive you nuts. If I spill, my life ain't worth a nickel.
Father Barry: And how much is your soul worth if you don't?

TAKE NOTE—Amazing combination of performances: Brando won Best Actor; Saint, Best Supporting Actress in her first film role; Cobb, Steiger, and Malden all nominated for Best Supporting Actor. Kazan won Best Director and the movie won Best Picture.

TRIVIA QUIZ—What is Terry Malloy's hobby in the movie? (Answer No. 62)

For evil to triumph, it is only necessary for good men to do nothing.
—EDMUND BURKE

Ordinary People

Drama 1980

Director: Robert Redford

Starring: Mary Tyler Moore, Donald Sutherland,
Timothy Hutton, Judd Hirsch, Elizabeth McGovern,
James B. Sikking

● ●

STORY CONCEPT—A family whose son is killed in a boating accident grows further apart. The young son attempts suicide because of guilt over his brother's death; he was on the boat with him and couldn't save him. The mother shows preference toward the older boy and has a problem showing her love to her husband and the younger son. The father feels caught in the middle and seeks therapy as has the younger son. Will the family survive?

THEME—The false belief that ignoring problems will cause them to go away only causes pain, and the problems get worse.

FAVORITE SCENE—Beth (Moore) awakens in the night and finds Calvin (Sutherland) sitting at the table weeping. He questions her love for him. She is unable to say the words "I love you." He admits his doubts about his love for her and his fear of the future without that love. Without a word, Beth goes upstairs and packs her bags.

MEMORABLE LINES—Father to Conrad (Hutton), the son: "Don't admire people too much! They'll disappoint you sometimes!"

TAKE NOTE—First film directed by Redford who wins Best Director. Best Supporting Actor for Hutton in his film debut. Best Picture award. Mary Tyler Moore's son commits suicide a month after the film is released.

TRIVIA QUIZ—What question by Calvin to Beth points out the weakness of partners in marriage? (Answer No. 63)

> *The tendency to seldom think of what we have but always of what we lack is the greatest tragedy on earth. Count your blessings—not your troubles!* —DALE CARNEGIE

The Paradine Case

Drama 1948

Director: Alfred Hitchcock

Starring: Gregory Peck, Ann Todd, Valli, Louis Jourdan, Charles Coburn, Charles Laughton

STORY CONCEPT—A very successful trial lawyer becomes obsessed with his beautiful client, Mrs. Paradine (Valli), who is accused of murdering her blind husband. Keane (Peck) is blinded to the truth and will not listen to his partner, Sir Simon (Coburn), nor his long-suffering wife, Gay (Todd).

THEME—A woman's beauty and charm sometimes blinds men to the reality of a situation.

FAVORITE SCENE—Gay Keane suggests to her husband, Anthony, that he needs to get away for a few days and relax. In fact, their anniversary is coming up. He drops a bombshell by his curt remark that some things are more important than anniversaries.

MEMORABLE LINES—Barrister Keane confers with his partner, Sir Simon, who suggests that Mrs. Paradine is the only real suspect in her husband's murder.

Keane: Well, there's a simple obvious fact. Mrs. Paradine is not a murderer: she's too fine a woman.
Simon: Indeed, I had the opinion that she was a woman of low estate and easy virtues.
Keane (blows up): You're an insufferable slob, incapable of recognizing genuine character!

TAKE NOTE—Leo G. Carroll, the counsel for the prosecution, has played in more Alfred Hitchcock movies than any other actor.

TRIVIA QUIZ—What are the words over the door to the courthouse where the trial takes place? (Answer No. 64)

> *Most of us keep one eye on the temptation we pray not to be led into.* —MARY H. WALDRIP

Patch Adams

Comedy/Drama 1998

Director: Tom Chadyac

Starring: Robin Williams, Monica Potter, Michael Jeter, Peter Coyote

● ●

STORY CONCEPT—A voluntary patient in a mental hospital finds he has a talent for making others laugh and forget their pain. He enrolls in medical school and the conflict begins between his philosophy and traditional medical practices, even though patients, nurses, and some medical professors appreciate the results he gets. His philosophy: "You treat a disease, you win, you lose. You treat a patient, I'll guarantee you'll win." This film is based on a true story.

THEME—Criticism is inevitable when new ideas challenge old.

FAVORITE SCENE—Patch (Williams) has a high-level discussion with his roommate Rudy (Jeter) when he learns that someone reported to the dean that he was cheating. Rudy denies it, but he's guilty because he is jealous of Patch who makes better grades. Later, they become good friends.

MEMORABLE LINES—Dean Anderson (Presnell) to Patch, who is always breaking the rules.

Dean: You think not all the rules apply to you.
Patch: But the golden rule does.

TAKE NOTE—Robin Williams and the cast and crew worked closely with the Make-A-Wish Foundation to fulfill the fantasies of several children who were at the time undergoing cancer treatment. The children appeared with Williams in scenes at the pediatric ward.

TRIVIA QUIZ—How did Patch reach an angry, rebellious patient (Coyote), who was dying of cancer, when no one else could? (Answer No. 65)

Laughter is a tranquilizer with no side effects.
—ARNOLD H. GLASOW

A Patch of Blue

Drama 1965

Director: Guy Green

Starring: Elizabeth Hartman, Sidney Poitier, Shelly Winters, Wallace Ford

• •

STORY CONCEPT—An eighteen-year-old blind girl lives with her prostitute mother and her drunkard grandfather. She is befriended by a young black man whom she meets in the park almost every day. She doesn't know it, but he becomes her ticket to freedom.

THEME—Hope meets kindness for the first time and love evolves.

FAVORITE SCENE— Selina (Hartman) spends her days cleaning the apartment, washing, ironing, and cooking for her mother (Winters) and "Ole Paw" (Ford). Mr. Faber, who pays her to string beads, takes her to the park one day. The introduction to the park opens up a new world of smells, sounds, and feelings. Selina, who was accidentally blinded by her mother when she was five, remembers that the sky is blue.

MEMORABLE LINES— In the city park, Gordon (Poitier), a young black, helps pick up some beads which Selina has accidentally scattered on the ground. He offers her pineapple juice. Delicious! The problem arises when her grandfather is late to pick her up and she doesn't know how to go to the restroom. The next day in the park with Gordon she refuses the juice. Gordon whispers: "There's a place just a few steps away where you can wash your hands (a delicate way of telling her about the restroom). Quickly, Selina says: "I would love some of that juice!"

TAKE NOTE—Hartman wears a pair of opaque contacts that not only make her appear blind, but genuinely deprive her of her sight.

TRIVIA QUIZ—What is the song Selina and Gordon whistle together in the park one day? (Answer No. 66)

> *So long as you can sweeten another's pain, life is not in vain.*
>
> —HELEN KELLER

Pride of the Yankees

Biography/Sports 1942

Director: Sam Wood

Starring: Gary Cooper, Teresa Wright, Walter Brennan, Elsa Janssen, Babe Ruth, Ludwig Stossel, Dan Duryea

STORY CONCEPT—Lou Gehrig, son of immigrants, becomes a major league baseball player and falls in love with the daughter of a baseball team owner. In the prime of life he is stricken with a deadly disease, ALS (now called Lou Gehrig's disease).

THEME—Ambition, hard work, and talent can bring much success; but disease is the great equalizer.

FAVORITE SCENE—Lou's (Cooper) mother (Janssen) attempts to take over the decorating of the apartment for the newlyweds. Lou puts a stop to this and tells his wife, Eleanor (Wright), that you can't run a household with two bosses.

MEMORABLE LINES—Over 62,000 people gather in Yankee Stadium in New York City to honor Lou Gehrig for his contribution to baseball. Lou responds: "People all say I've had a bad break; but today, today I consider myself the luckiest man on the face of the earth."

TAKE NOTE—Lou Gehrig held the record of most consecutive games played for over fifty years (2130 over 14-year period). He took himself out of the game because this unknown disease was hindering him from playing his best.

TRIVIA QUIZ—When Eleanor first meets Lou she calls him a little puppy. What kind? (Answer No. 67)

> *You count on it, you rely on it to buffer the passage of time, to keep the memory of sunshine and high skies alive, and then, just when the days are all twilight, when you need it most, it stops.*
>
> —A. BARTLETT GIAMATTI, *Baseball Commissioner and former president of Yale University*

Quiz Show
Drama 1994

Director: Robert Redford

Starring: John Turturro, Mira Sorvino, Rob Morrow,
Ralph Fiennes, Paul Scofield, David Paymer

• •

STORY CONCEPT—An unpolished blue-collar worker and an intellectual white-collar college professor find themselves in the same boat as they participate in the deception of a quiz show in the late '50s. A congressional investigator gathers the evidence to bring the show down, although he becomes good friends with the professor. The producer of the show justifies the cheating by saying: "We are in show business and this is what the people want." Based on a true story.

THEME—People have a tendency to justify their actions one way or another because they don't like to look at the truth.

FAVORITE SCENE—College professor Charles Van Doren (Fiennes) agonizes as he reveals to his upright and ethical father, Mark Van Doren (Scofield), that the program is rigged and he has compromised his principles. The elder Van Doren, a member of one of America's great literary families, is devastated and speechless.

MEMORABLE LINES—Congressional investigator, Dick Goodvin (Morrow), shares with Charles Van Doren, his new friend: "My uncle had an affair eight years ago. He told his wife. I asked him why and he said: 'The getting-away-with-it part I couldn't live with!'"

TAKE NOTE—Robert Redford, the director, said that he watched this quiz show on TV during his tenure at acting school and he could tell that the real Charles Van Doren on that show was acting.

TRIVIA QUIZ—What is the name of the rigged quiz show in this movie? (Answer No. 68)

> *Glass, china and reputation are easily cracked and never well mended.* —BENJAMIN FRANKLIN

Raiders Of The Lost Ark

Adventure 1981

Director: Steven Spielberg

Starring: Harrison Ford, Karen Allen, Ronald Lacey, John Rhys-Davies

STORY CONCEPT—Indiana Jones (Ford), an archeologist and adventurer, learns that the Nazis are searching for the Ark of the Covenant, the box which cradles the Ten Commandments given by Moses to the Jewish people. He never resists a challenge to discover a relic of the past. The adventure begins, and it's a roller coaster ride that will keep you on the edge of your seat! Buckle up!

THEME—Risk-taking is a stepping stone to life-expanding discoveries.

FAVORITE SCENE The Nazis capture the Ark of the Covenant and are transporting it by truck. Indiana Jones pursues the Nazis on horseback, in a jeep he captures, and then on a motorcycle. In his attempt to stop the truck he almost gets run down and ends up being dragged on the ground by the truck.

MEMORABLE LINES—Prior to the big chase scene:

Jones: I'm going after that truck!
Sallah: (Rhys-Davies) How?
Jones: I don't know, I'm making this up as I go!

TAKE NOTE—Ford was questioned about actually being dragged behind the truck. "Were you worried?" "No," Ford quipped. "If it really were dangerous they would have filmed more of the movie first!"

TRIVIA QUIZ—What is the penalty in the Bible for touching the Ark of the Covenant without God's approval? (Answer No. 69)

Life has no romance without risk. —SARAH DOHERTY (*the first one-legged person to scale Mt. McKinley*)

Rain Man

Drama 1988

Director: Barry Levinson

Starring: Dustin Hoffman, Tom Cruise, Valeria Golino

STORY CONCEPT—A self-centered young man finds that his wealthy father has died and left an inheritance to a brother he did not know he had. This relationship story begins when he takes his middle-aged autistic savant brother from an institution and they set out on a cross-country journey of discovery.

THEME—A person's search for riches may end with a truer wealth he is not looking for.

FAVORITE SCENE—Charlie Babbitt (Cruise) questions Raymond Babbitt (Hoffman), his newly-found brother, about his past and learns that the "rain man" of his childhood was really Raymond.

MEMORABLE LINES—Raymond and Charlie eat breakfast at the coffee shop where Raymond's gift of memory is discovered. The waitress approaches.

Raymond (looks at her name tag): Sally Dibbs. Dibbs Sally. 461-0192.
Sally: How did you know my phone number?
Charlie: How did you know that?
Raymond: You said to read the telephone book last night. Dibbs Sally. 461-0192.
Charlie: He, uh, remembers things. Little things sometimes.
Sally: Very clever boys. I'll be right back.

TAKE NOTE—After being interviewed by the psychiatrist, Raymond leans his head against Charlie and says "My main man, Charlie." This was unscripted, and improvised by Hoffman.

TRIVIA QUIZ—What are Raymond's two favorite TV shows? (Answer No. 70)

> *The smallest package we have ever seen is a man all wrapped up in himself.* —FREDONIA, NY Censor

Rear Window

Thriller/Romance 1954

Director: Alfred Hitchcock

Starring: Jimmy Stewart, Grace Kelly, Thelma Ritter, Wendell Corey, Raymond Burr

● ●

STORY CONCEPT—A society beauty loves a photographer who attempts to talk her out of marriage while he is laid up with his leg in a cast. From the large rear window of his apartment he views people in adjoining apartments and suspects a man has murdered his wife. He cannot investigate personally, so he enlists the help of his eager girlfriend and the police who have no evidence to follow.

THEME—You sometimes see the faults of others when you will not see your own.

FAVORITE SCENE—Lisa Freemont (Kelly) gets into the suspect's room and is searching for clues to a murder when the suspect opens the door and surprises her. L. B. Jeffries (Stewart) is watching from his apartment and can do nothing to warn her.

MEMORABLE LINES—Stella (Ritter), Jeffries' maid, rebukes him: "We've become a race of Peeping Toms. What people ought to do is get outside their own house and look in for a change. Yes sir. How's that for a bit of homespun philosophy?"

TAKE NOTE—In 1954, this movie set was the largest indoor set built at Paramount Studios and every scene was shot from inside the Jeffries' apartment, giving the viewer of the movie the same impressions Jeffries experiences.

TRIVIA QUIZ—What book is Lisa reading at the conclusion of the movie, and what magazine does she exchange it for when she sees L. B. has fallen asleep? (Answer No. 73)

The moment someone says 'this is very risky' it becomes attractive to me. —KATE CAPSHAW

Red River

Western 1948

Director: Howard Hawks

Starring: John Wayne, Montgomery Clift, Joanne Dru,
Walter Brennan, Coleen Gray, John Ireland

STORY CONCEPT—A cattle baron drives his cattle to Red River when his adopted son turns against him because of his tyranny. The rancher who loses his herd seeks revenge on the person he loves the most.

THEME—A self-centered life often leads to a life of loneliness.

FAVORITE SCENE—Tom Dunson (Wayne) tracks his adopted son, Matt Garth (Clift), to a wagon train and learns that Matt had been there eight days before. Tom has a conversation with Tess Millay (Dru) who has fallen in love with Matt. He offers her a strange proposal which she rejects.

MEMORABLE LINES—Tom Dunson was a man who ruled with a gun. He would kill a man, sometimes justifiably, sometimes not. In essence, he would be his judge, jury, undertaker, and preacher. One of his cowhands remarks: "Plantin' and readin', planting and readin' (the Bible). Fill a man full o' lead, stick him in the ground an' then read words on him. Why, when you've killed a man, why try to read the Lord in as a partner on the job?" (But the cowhand never said this to his face.)

TAKE NOTE—Texas Longhorn cattle had been nearly extinct as a breed for about 50 years when this film was made. Only a few dozen animals were available. In the herd scenes, most of the cattle were Hereford with the Longhorns prominently displayed when the cameras were close up.

TRIVIA QUIZ—Which star who had never ridden a horse before appears in his first film? (Answer No. 71)

> *Bitterness is the poison we swallow while hoping the other person dies.* —SKIP GRAY

84

Regarding Henry

Drama 1991

Director: Mike Nichols

Starring: Harrison Ford, Annette Bening, Mikki Allen,
John MacKay

STORY CONCEPT—A big-shot, ruthless lawyer is shot in the head and almost dies. He has to learn to eat, talk, walk, and read all over again. With the love of his wife and daughter, he slowly recovers and finds he does not fit into his former life as a cold-hearted attorney and cheating husband.

THEME—There is hope for a man who humbles himself to depend on others.

FAVORITE SCENE—Henry Turner (Ford) is reluctant to leave the rehabilitation center until his daughter, Rachel (Allen), helps him tie his shoes. He asks her how she learned to tie shoes. She responds that he taught her. This gives him the confidence to go home.

MEMORABLE LINES—Henry gets depressed when he finds out his law firm is corrupt, so he calls Bradley (MacKay), his therapist, at the rehab center:

Henry: I don't like who I was.
Bradley: My knees are bad. Why? Football was my life until I busted my knees. What else was there for me? Life was over. But it was a test. I had to find a new life. I wanted to have the life of the therapist who treated me. That's how I came to help you. You'll figure out who you are.

TAKE NOTE—Would you believe that a man learning to read again could tackle and comprehend complicated legal briefs? Yet that is what Ford does in this movie.

TRIVIA QUIZ—What wish of his daughter does Henry unknowingly fulfill? (Answer No. 72)

Life is full of endings, but every ending is a new beginning.
                                                            —ANONYMOUS

85

Rocky
Drama/Sports 1976

Director: John Avildson

Starring: Sylvester Stallone, Talia Shire, Burt Young, Burgess Meredith, Carl Weathers

• •

STORY CONCEPT— Rocky Balboa (Stallone) is a down-on-his-luck boxer with a low self-image. He is given a chance to make it big, in a match against the reigning champion, Apollo Creed (Weathers).

THEME— The underdog struggles against all odds to attain the impossible and succeeds.

FAVORITE SCENE—Adrian (Shire), who works in the corner pet shop, finally agrees to a date with Rocky. He comes to her home and she is so painfully shy that she won't come out of her room. Finally, Rocky convinces her to come out and go for a walk. It is an awkward situation because neither of them knows how to relate to the opposite sex.

MEMORABLE LINES—Adrian's brother, Paulie (Young), a pitiful fellow who browbeats his sister, talking to Rocky:

Paulie: Why do you like my sister?
Rocky: She's got gaps, I've got gaps. We fill in the gaps.

TAKE NOTE—Stallone wrote the script for this story in three days after he saw Mohammed Ali beat Chuck Wepner who went the distance. He kept it for several years and would not sell it unless the buyer agreed for him to play the lead role. The film was shot in 28 days. It won Best Picture.

TRIVIA QUIZ—How old were Rocky and Adrian in the movie? (Answer No. 74)

> *Inside of a ring or out, ain't nothing wrong with going down. It's staying down that's wrong.* —MOHAMMED ALI

Roman Holiday

Comedy/Romance 1953

Director: William Wyler

Starring: Audrey Hepburn, Gregory Peck, Eddie Albert

STORY CONCEPT—A lonely princess visiting Rome decides her life is too restricted and runs away for a day. She meets an American reporter who serves as her guide, and they fall for each other.

THEME—A life of nobility forfeits freedoms others take for granted.

FAVORITE SCENE—Princess Anne (Hepburn), Joe Bradley (Peck), the reporter, and Irving Radovich (Albert), the photographer, visit the grotesque statue of truth. Joe warns Princess Anne that if she puts her hand in the mouth of the creature and tells the truth she will not be harmed. She is reluctant, but Joe thrusts his hand in and pulls it out quickly. She squeals with fright because she can't see his hand.

MEMORABLE LINES—In an interview with Princess Anne by reporters after her day of fun in Rome with Bradley:

Reporter: And what, in the opinion of Your Highness, is the outlook for a friendship among nations?
Princess: I have every faith in it—as I have faith in relations between people.
Bradley: May I say, speaking for my own (pause) press service, we believe Your Highness's faith will not be unjustified.
Princess: I am so glad to hear you say it. (She smiles with relief as Irving hands her the photographs he had taken.)

TAKE NOTE—The scene in which Peck pretends that his hand is bitten off in the mouth of the statue was ad-libbed, and Hepburn's response was genuine.

TRIVIA QUIZ—Who won an Oscar in this film in their first leading role? (Answer No. 15)

Enjoying each other's good is heaven begun. —LUCY C. SMITH

87

Schindler's List

Biography/War 1993

Director: Steven Spielberg
Starring: Liam Neeson, Ben Kingsley, Ralph Fiennes

● ●

STORY CONCEPT—Oskar Schindler, an egotistical and immoral man, shows great acts of human kindness toward Jews during World War II in Poland where thousands were being imprisoned and slaughtered. Based on a true story.

THEME—Kindness is a drop of humanity in an ocean of inhumanity.

FAVORITE SCENE—Factory owner Schindler (Neeson) says good-bye to the Jewish workers for the last time. After announcing the end of the war, he looks at his car and weeps openly because he could have sold the car to save more lives.

MEMORABLE LINES—Schindler to Amon Goethe (Fiennes), camp commander, a madman who kills for sport:

Schindler: Power is when we have every justification to kill, and we don't.
Goethe: You think that's power?
Schindler: That's what the Emperor said. A man stole something, he's brought in before the Emperor, he throws himself down on the ground. He begs for his life, he knows he's going to die. And the Emperor (pause) pardons him. It's a worthless man, he lets him go.
Goethe: I think you are drunk.
Schindler: That's power, Amon. That is power.

TAKE NOTE—Director Spielberg was not allowed to film inside Auschwitz, so the scenes of the death camp were filmed outside the gates on a set constructed as a mirror image of the real location.

TRIVIA QUIZ—From what is the gift made that the factory workers give to Schindler? (Answer No. 76)

And whoever gives one of these little ones only a cup of cold water ... shall by no means lose his reward. —JESUS

Seven Days in May
Thriller/Drama 1964

Director: John Frankenheimer

Starring: Burt Lancaster, Kirk Douglas, Fredric March, Ava Gardner, Edmond O'Brien, Martin Balsam

● ●

STORY CONCEPT—A general of the U.S. Army leads a coup against an unpopular president because he is in favor of disarmament, and he feels this threatens the nation's security. One of the general's aides learns of the secret attempt and notifies the president. The wheels of democracy begin to grind.

THEME—One basic element in our Constitution is civilian control of the military.

FAVORITE SCENE—When President Lyman (March) hears of the secret plan to take over, he meets with General Scott (Lancaster), who is spearheading it. Scott demands the president's resignation because he has disgraced the office by his weak position on security. President Lyman retorts by demanding that if he wants the office, then run for it. He demands General Scott's resignation.

MEMORABLE LINES—General Scott to Colonel Martin (Douglas), his aide, when he learns that the incriminating evidence was released by his own aide:

Scott: Do you know who Judas in the Bible was?
Martin: Yes, I know who Judas was. He's the man I worked for and admired until he disgraced the four stars on his uniform.

TAKE NOTE—The three main actors in this movie have a total of 137 years in films: March (44), Lancaster (45), and Douglas, (48).

TRIVIA QUIZ—What did the president say would be the impact of a military take-over of the country? (Answer No. 77)

> When you see a rattlesnake poised to strike, you do not wait until he has struck before you crush him. —FRANKLIN DELANO ROOSEVELT, 32nd U.S. President

89

Shadowlands

Drama/Romance 1993

Director: Richard Attenborough

Starring: Anthony Hopkins, Debra Winger,
Edward Hardwicke, Joseph Mazello

● ●

STORY CONCEPT—C. S. Lewis (Hopkins), author of the Narnia books and others, and a bachelor of many years, entertains a fan from the states, Mrs. Joy Gresham (Winger), a poet, and her small son, Douglas (Mazello). Their encounter turns into a seven-year relationship and a marriage that ends with Joy's death. His teaching at Oxford and lectures on suffering are changed by this tragedy.

THEME—The road of life travels from happiness to great sorrow, but it's the only road we have.

FAVORITE SCENE—Jack attempts to comfort Douglas in the attic after Joy's death. Douglas reveals that he doesn't believe in heaven. Jack assures him that it's all right to believe that. Both of them express their desire to see Joy again. Jack breaks down, sobbing uncontrollably, and the two of them embrace.

MEMORABLE LINES—Joy to Jack, when she is very ill:

Joy: Jack, you always say real life hasn't begun yet. You better be right!

Joy (on another occasion): We can't have the happiness of yesterday without the pain of today. That's the deal.

TAKE NOTE—Jack (C. S. Lewis) never learned to drive, although he attempted to learn many times. In the movie, however, he drives an automobile.

TRIVIA QUIZ—What is difficult for Lewis, a prolific writer, to express in words? (Answer No. 78)

> *I know God will not give me anything I cannot handle. I just wish he didn't trust me so much.* —MOTHER TERESA

Shane
Western 1953

Director: George Stevens

Starring: Alan Ladd, Jean Arthur, Van Heflin,
Brandon De Wilde, Jack Palance, Ben Johnson

STORY CONCEPT—Shane (Ladd) is a retired gunfighter who comes to the aid of a homestead family terrorized by a cattle baron and his hired gun.

THEME—The decent life, though difficult, can be admired by those who have given their lives to unworthy ventures.

FAVORITE SCENE—The first night Shane stays with Joe (Heflin), Mariam (Arthur), and their son, Joey (DeWilde), he envies their lifestyle and Joey is captivated by him. The parents see a difficulty here because they want Joey to live a non-violent life unlike the life of Shane.

MEMORABLE LINES—Shane to Ryker, the wicked cattle baron:

Shane: Your kind of days are over.
Ryker: My days! What about yours, gunfighter?
Shane: The difference is I know it!

TAKE NOTE—Jack Palance, who plays the hired gunfighter, did not like horses. He only mounted a horse well one time in the movie and that scene was not used. The part where he walks his horse into town the first time was not originally planned that way, but due to his noticeably unsteady riding manner, the director kept it in the film. It has become a classic scene in movie history.

TRIVIA QUIZ—What unpopular drink for gunfighters does Shane order at the bar? (Answer No. 79)

I fear there will be no future for those who do not change.
—LOUIS L'AMOUR

We run away all the time to avoid coming face to face with ourselves. —ANONYMOUS

The Shawshank Redemption
Drama 1994

Director: Frank Darabont

Starring: Tim Robbins, Morgan Freeman, Bob Gunton, Clancy Brown, James Whitmore

STORY CONCEPT—A banker, Andy Dufresne (Robbins), accused of murdering his wife, has to deal with brutal inmates and his own despair when he's sentenced to life in Shawshank Prison. With a new friend, Red Redding (Freeman), a hustler who can get most anything for a price, Andy prepares for his ticket to freedom.

THEME—Justice delayed is not always justice denied.

FAVORITE SCENE—Andy, Red, and some of the other inmates are spreading black tar on the prison roof when they overhear Captain Hadley (Brown) talk about inheriting $35,000, and complain about the heavy taxes. Andy offers to help him out with the situation. Hadley accepts Andy's offer, but not before he almost kills him.

MEMORABLE LINES—After a month in solitary, Andy talks to Red about the music he hears in his head and heart.

Red: I had a harmonica once, but I don't play anymore.
Andy: Here's where it makes the most sense. You need it so you don't forget. Forget that there are places in the world that aren't made out of stone. That there's something inside that's yours, that they can't touch.

TAKE NOTE—The American Society for the Prevention of Cruelty to Animals monitored the filming of scenes involving Brooks' (Whitmore) crow. During the scenes where he fed it a maggot, the society objected on the grounds that it was cruel to the maggot, and required that they use a maggot that had died from natural causes. One was found, and the scene was filmed.

TRIVIA QUIZ—What did a picture of Rita Hayworth have to do with the movie? (Answer No. 80)

If you can't fight, and you can't flee, flow. —ROBERT ELIOT

Singin' in the Rain
Musical/Comedy 1952

Directors: Gene Kelly and Stanley Donen

Starring: Gene Kelly, Donald O'Connor, Debbie Reynolds, Jean Hagen

●●●●●●●●●●●●●●●●●●●●●●●●●●●●●●●●●●●●

STORY CONCEPT—A famous romantic couple in silent films makes the transition to a musical; there's only one problem—she can't sing and she can't talk! A young actress, Kathy Seldon (Reynolds), is brought in to dub her voice and Don Lockwood (Kelly) falls in love with her.

THEME—People look for ways to express their happiness, like singing and dancing.

FAVORITE SCENE—Don Lockwood and Lina Lamont (Hagan) are rehearsing for their first talking movie, and Lina's voice is so shrill it could shatter glass. Besides, she keeps moving her mouth from side to side and only half the words are heard over the stationary microphone hidden in the flowers.

MEMORABLE LINES

Lina (in a high, squeaky voice): "What's wrong with the way I talk? What's the big idea? Am I dumb or something?" (Everyone is afraid to answer that question.)

TAKE NOTE—Gene Kelly has a 103-degree temperature when he dances in the rain. The rain is water mixed with milk, and it caused his wool suit to shrink.

TRIVIA QUIZ—What is the name of Cosmo Brown's (O'Connor) hilarious, acrobatic song and dance routine? (Answer No. 81)

> *Enjoy yourself. These are the 'good old days' you're going to miss in the years ahead.* —ANONYMOUS

Sister Act

Comedy 1992

Director: Emile Ardolino

Starring: Whoopi Goldberg, Maggie Smith, Harvey Keitel, Kathy Najimy, Wendy Makkena, Mary Wickes

● ●

STORY CONCEPT—Deloris Van Cortier (Goldberg), a Reno night-club singer, sees her boyfriend, Vince LaRocca (Keitel), commit a murder. She becomes a fugitive, and the police hide her in a convent. Her musical talent gets her appointed choir director and new music fills the pews in a dying inner-city church.

THEME—Exposure to a better way of life creates an atmosphere that makes it easier to become a better person.

FAVORITE SCENE—Deloris (aka Sister Mary Clarence) is introduced to the choir at practice and they sound like screech owls. Because of her background in music she is asked to assist. She reluctantly accepts and begins with the basic do-re-mi's, bringing pleasing results which she attributes to the original instructor. The instructor is pleased.

MEMORABLE LINES—During a raid on the freezer for ice cream, three members of the choir, Mary Patrick (Najimy), Mary Robert (Makkena), and Mary Lazarus (Wickes), question Deloris about her stability in staying with the choir.

Deloris: We gonna always be together.
Mary Lazarus: That's what Diana Ross said!

TAKE NOTE—Whoopi Goldberg sang her own songs in the movie after thirty hours of practice.

TRIVIA QUIZ—With what famous brand ice cream did the nuns treat Deloris? (Answer No. 82)

There's a period of life when we swallow a knowledge of ourselves and it becomes either good or sour inside. —PEARL BAILEY

Sounder

Drama 1972

Director: Martin Ritt

Starring: Cicely Tyson, Paul Winfield, Kevin Hooks, Taj Mahal, James Best

STORY CONCEPT—A black sharecropper family in Louisiana in 1933 sees their breadwinner, Nathan Lee Morgan (Winfield), arrested and taken to a prison camp because he stole food on one occasion to keep his family from starving. His wife, Rebecca (Tyson), sends the oldest son, David Lee (Hooks), to visit his father. On the way, he meets a dedicated black school teacher and gets a glimpse of a better life to come.

THEME—The hope of a better tomorrow is powerful medicine.

FAVORITE SCENE—The Morgan children awaken to the sounds and smell of bacon frying and eggs scrambling after eating practically nothing for a long time. They run and squeal and shout and laugh!

MEMORABLE LINES—David Lee's father is handicapped. He wants to stay home and help, but his father insists that he go away to school: "You lose some of the time what you go after, but you lose all of the time what you don't go after."

TAKE NOTE—This movie gets its name from the family dog, Sounder, who represents the persevering human spirit, protective of his family, nursing his wounds, and returning to the family he loves and who loves him.

TRIVIA QUIZ—How long is Nathan Lee sentenced for stealing food? (Answer No. 83)

> *Gnaw your own bone; gnaw at it, bury it, unearth, gnaw it still.*
> —HENRY DAVID THOREAU

Superman
Fantasy/Adventure 1978

Director: Richard Lester

Starring: Christopher Reeve, Margot Kidder, Gene Hackman, Ned Beatty, Jackie Cooper, Marlon Brando

• •

STORY CONCEPT—An orphaned baby from the planet of Krypton is sent to earth and grows into Clark Kent (Reeve), a man with superhuman power, whose mission in life is to use that power for good and against evil.

THEME—The person who achieves his potential for good is to be greatly admired.

FAVORITE SCENE—Superman takes Lois for a free-flying flight through the skies and then gives her an exclusive interview on the balcony of her penthouse apartment.

MEMORABLE LINES—Clark saves Lois from a robber:

Clark: Really, Lois, supposing that man had shot you? Is it worth risking your life over ten dollars, two credit cards, a hairbrush, and a lipstick?
Lois: How did you know that?
Clark: Know what?
Lois: You just described the exact contents of my purse.
Clark: Hmm. Lucky guess.

TAKE NOTE—Marlon Brando (Jor-El), Superman's original father, received $4 million for his ten minutes on screen.

TRIVIA QUIZ—What famous star with forty years experience plays the part of Mr. Kent, Clark's foster father? (Answer No. 84)

> If a man has a talent and cannot use it, he has failed. If he has a talent and uses only half of it, he has partly failed. If he has a talent and learns somehow to use the whole of it, he has gloriously succeeded, and won a satisfaction and a triumph few men ever know. —THOMAS WOLFE

Tender Mercies

Drama 1983

Director: Bruce Beresford

Starring: Robert Duvall, Tess Harper, Allan Hubbard,
Betty Buckley, Ellen Barkin, Wilford Brimley

STORY CONCEPT—A broken-down country singer and songwriter gives up the bottle and takes a job as a hired hand at a motel for a widow who lives alone with her son. The love of this lady and her son puts him back on the right track.

THEME—Loving and tender mercy bring out the best in folks.

FAVORITE SCENE—Mac Sledge (Duvall) comes home early from attending the concert of his ex-wife, Dixie (Buckley), a country music star who won't let him see his daughter. His new wife, Rosa Lee (Harper), doesn't understand why and she's jealous.

MEMORABLE LINES—Mac's eighteen-year-old daughter comes to see him for the first time in eight years.

Sue Anne: She told me she'd have me arrested if I ever tried to see you. Did you really try to kill her once?
Mac: Yes, I did. I got mad and was drinking.
Sue Anne: You think you ever will sing again.
Mac: I think about it.
Sue Anne: You used to sing to me about a dove—on the wings of a dove.
Mac: I don't remember that.
(She leaves. Mac goes to the window and begins singing "On the wings of a snow white dove . . .")

TAKE NOTE—Duvall wrote two and sings all of the songs himself.

TRIVIA QUIZ—Who makes their film debut in *Tender Mercies*? (Answer No. 85)

> *When God is at your side, He helps you face the music, even when you don't like the tune.* —JOHN L. MASON

The Thing from Another World
Thriller/Science Fiction 1951

Director: Christian Nyby

Starring: Kenneth Tobey, Margaret Sheridan, Dewey Martin

STORY CONCEPT—Conflict arises between the military and some scientists at the North Pole when an alien is found in a block of ice. The scientists want to study and examine it, but before this can be done it accidentally thaws and becomes a threat. The military wants to seek and destroy the alien before it destroys them. A battle ensues between two world intelligences—this world and the world of outer space.

THEME—Man's greatest enemy is the fear of the unknown.

FAVORITE SCENE—The climactic encounter between the alien and the earthlings occurs when a plan is devised to destroy the creature which has all the characteristics of a vegetable. When seen for the first time, it comes through a door, and a flame-thrower pushes it back. Ned Scott, the reporter, complains that the door wasn't open long enough to get pictures. When they ask if he wants it opened again, he emphatically answers no!!

MEMORABLE LINES—The military at the North Pole attempt to thaw out a space ship seen beneath the ice. An explosion occurs, and Scotty remarks, "So few people can boast that they lost a man from Mars and a flying saucer all in the same day? What if Columbus had discovered America, then mislaid it?"

TAKE NOTE—This movie was made in an ice house. It was very successful at the box office although no one in it received over $500 a week.

TRIVIA QUIZ—Who plays the role of The Thing? (Answer No. 86)

He has not learned the lesson of life who does not every day surmount a fear. —RALPH WALDO EMERSON

98

3:10 to Yuma

Western 1957

Director: Delmer Daves

Starring: Van Heflin, Glenn Ford, Leora Dana, Felicia Farr,
Henry Jones, Richard Jaeckel

● ●

STORY CONCEPT—An outlaw leader, Ben Wade (Ford), is captured but his gang is still on the prowl. Drought-stricken rancher Dan Evans (Heflin) needs money and is persuaded to escort Wade in secret to a nearby town with a railway station, where they will board the train to stand trial in Yuma.

THEME—People of low standing sometimes have the highest principles.

FAVORITE SCENE—Wade and Evans get an upstairs room in the hotel where they wait for the train. Wade's gang arrives in town and Wade appears confident they will rescue him. Evans' friend, Alex Potter (Jones), the town drunk and the only one with courage to help him, is shot by the gang on the street. Wade attempts to psyche out Evans and offers him large sums of money. The pressure mounts as the minutes pass. How can he safely get them to the train?

MEMORABLE LINES—The marshal to a reluctant posse on guarding the outlaw, Wade: "Safe? Who knows what's safe? I knew a man who died looking at his wife. My own grandmother fought Indians for sixty years and choked to death on lemon pie!"

TAKE NOTE—Glenn Ford was offered the role of the rancher, but chose to play the outlaw instead.

TRIVIA QUIZ—What is the serendipity Evans and his family receive at the end of the movie? (Answer No. 87)

Courage is being scared to death, but saddling up anyway.

—JOHN WAYNE

To Kill a Mockingbird
Drama 1962

Director: Robert Mulligan

Starring: Gregory Peck, Mary Badham, Phillip Alford, Brock Peters, Robert Duvall

STORY CONCEPT—Atticus Finch (Peck), a Southern lawyer, defends Tom Robinson (Peters), a black man, against an undeserved charge: the rape of a pitiful white woman. The story is told through the eyes of his daughter, Scout (Badham). A classic.

THEME—A man who stands for fairness against public opinion endures suffering.

FAVORITE SCENE—Atticus stands night guard at the jail house where Tom Robinson is secured, as a mob with violence in their eyes gathers outside. Atticus' children show up, and Scout walks through the crowd to her father's side. He insists that she leave, but she begins innocently questioning the men in a harmless manner, which in the end convicts them. They walk away in shame with their heads bowed.

MEMORABLE LINES—Atticus speaks to his ten-year-old son, Jem, after he has a frightening experience with a drunk: "There are a lot of ugly things in this world. I wish I could keep them away from you. But that's not possible."

TAKE NOTE—The pocket watch used in the movie belonged to author Harper Lee's own father. She later gave the watch to Gregory Peck because he reminded her so much of her father. (Lee wrote the book of the same title on which this movie is based.)

TRIVIA QUIZ—What famous actor plays Boo Radley in this movie, his first role? (Answer No. 88)

> *There are many ways to measure success, not the least of which is the way your child describes you when talking to a friend.*
>
> —ANONYMOUS

Tootsie
Comedy/Romance 1982

Director: Sydney Pollack

Starring: Dustin Hoffman, Teri Garr, Jessica Lange, Charles Durning, Bill Murray, Dabney Coleman, George Gaynes, Geena Davis, Sydney Pollack

• •

STORY CONCEPT—A struggling actor with an attitude disguises himself as a woman and finally lands a role in a TV soap opera. Amazingly, he receives great acclaim and becomes a more sensitive, caring person in the process.

THEME—Successful relationships are based on honesty and friendship.

FAVORITE SCENE—Dorothy (Hoffman) is invited to spend the weekend in the home of Julie (Lange), the leading actress in the soap opera. Dorothy (aka Michael Dorsey) wants to get to know her better, but spends his time fighting off the advances of her father, Les (Durning).

MEMORABLE LINES—Michael to his agent, George (Pollack):

Michael: Are you saying that no one in New York will work with me?
George: No, no, that's too limited. No one in Hollywood wants to work with you either. I can't even send you up for a commercial. You played a tomato and they still went a half day over schedule because you wouldn't sit down.

TAKE NOTE—Dustin Hoffman suggested the title of this movie because his mother called him Tootsie when he was a child.

TRIVIA QUIZ—Who made their film debut in Tootsie? (Answer No. 89)

O what a tangled web we weave, when first we practice to deceive.
—SIR WALTER SCOTT

To Sir with Love
Drama 1967

Director: James Clavell

Starring: Sidney Poitier, Judy Geeson, Suzy Kendall

● ●

STORY CONCEPT—An unemployed engineer from the West Indies turns to teaching in the London slums. It's his first assignment. By example, he teaches them to talk civil to one another and practice courtesy. They put the books aside and discuss practical matters: sex, marriage, and getting a job.

THEME—Exposure to a variety of experiences can open up the opportunity to grow in one's life.

FAVORITE SCENE—Mark Thackeray (Poitier) visits the home of a student whose black mother has died and finds all of his students, who had declared they would not go, already there.

MEMORABLE LINES—Mark has received an offer from an engineering firm and he plans to leave teaching. At the end-of-term dance a fellow teacher says: "If you must leave, go to another school. Don't waste time on electronics. (Pause) Oh, I swore I wouldn't interfere." (Mark tears up the offer and stays on.)

TAKE NOTE—Twelve years before this film was made, Poitier played the part of an unruly student, with Glenn Ford as a teacher, in *The Blackboard Jungle*.

TRIVIA QUIZ—What is the name of the hit song Lulu (a professional singer) sings in the movie? (Answer No. 90)

> *Never tell a young person that something cannot be done. God may have been waiting for centuries for somebody ignorant enough of the impossible to do that thing.* —DR. J. A. HOLMES

The Train
Drama/War 1964

Director: John Frankenheimer
Starring: Burt Lancaster, Paul Scofield, Jeanne Moreau

● ●

STORY CONCEPT—French Resistance fighters are sabotaging trains in German-occupied France. Nazi Colonel von Waldheim (Scofield) attempts to take the art collections of France to Germany. Resistance leaders are requested to keep this train from being destroyed and from reaching its destination.

THEME—A person and his heritage are not easily separated.

FAVORITE SCENE—Labiche (Lancaster), a French railway official, pleads for the life of Papa Bolle (Simon), an elderly engineer, who has sabotaged his own train in order to give the Allies time to bomb the railway center.

MEMORABLE LINES—Labiche, also a Resistance fighter, argues with the curator of the museum over saving the paintings.

Labiche: I won't waste lives on paintings.
Curator: They wouldn't be wasted. Excuse me, I know that's a terrible thing to say, but those paintings are part of France. The Germans want to take them away. They've taken our land, our food, they live in our houses, and now they're trying to take our art. This beauty, this vision of life, born out of France, our special vision, our trust—we hold it in trust, don't you see, for everyone? This is our pride, what we create and hold for the world. There are worse things to risk your life for than that.

TAKE NOTE—*The Train* is based on historical reality. Four locomotives, forty cars, and an entire station are actually destroyed in the explosions and collisions. Lancaster, a former circus acrobat, performs his own film stunts.

TRIVIA QUIZ—With what small object does Papa Bolle delay the progress of the locomotive? (Answer No. 92)

Next to excellence is the appreciation of it. —THACKERAY

The Treasure of the Sierra Madre
Western 1948

Director: John Huston

Starring: Humphrey Bogart, Walter Huston, Tim Holt, Bruce Bennett

● ●

STORY CONCEPT—Two down-and-outs join up with an old prospector to search for gold in Mexico. They encounter bandits, strangers, extreme heat, and hardships, but they find their gold—only to find that it begins to possess them and they turn into suspicious, untrusting misers.

THEME—Relations with money reveals the true character of a person.

FAVORITE SCENE—Fred C. Dobbs (Bogart), Bob (Holt), and Howard (Huston) read the letter of the stranger, Cody (Bennett), who has been killed by bandits. The letter, which tells of his wife and family, motivates two of them to want to share their wealth with her.

MEMORABLE LINES—Prospector Howard talks about gold:

Howard: Gold is a very devilish sort of thing. It changes your character completely. The more you have the more you want to add.
Dobbs: That'll never happen to me.
Howard: I know what gold does to men's souls.

TAKE NOTE—This was the first American movie to be shot entirely on location outside the U.S. The financial backers of the movie were nervous: a movie with no sex, and Mexicans speaking Spanish? Voted No. 30 by the American Film Institute.

TRIVIA QUIZ—What causes the Indians to treat Howard like a god? (Answer No. 91)

> *Experience is a hard teacher, because she gives the test first, the lesson afterward.* —VERNON LAW

The Trip to Bountiful
Drama 1985

Director: Peter Masterson

Starring: Geraldine Page, John Heard, Carlin Glynn, Rebecca DeMornay, Richard Bradford

● ●

STORY CONCEPT—An elderly widow has problems coping with life in her married son's home in the city. She decides to visit her home town without notifying anyone. The search for her and the encounter could be the basis for a better relationship between her and her family.

THEME—Change is difficult for young and old alike but it is sometimes necessary.

FAVORITE SCENE—Mrs. Watts (Page), an unhappy widow, makes it back to her old home town after a 20-year absence. Her daughter-in-law, Jessie Mae (Glynn), is furious because she has run away. Jessie Mae confronts her with some written rules to abide by if they are to live in the same house. Her son, Ludie (Heard), having never crossed his wife before, gives an unwritten rule of his own in high volume language.

MEMORABLE LINES—Mrs. Watts explains to her bus companion, Thelma (DeMornay), the nature of her daughter-in-law whom Thelma met briefly at the bus station when they left: "Jessie Mae thinks everybody is crazy who doesn't want to sit in a beauty parlor all day or drink Coca Cola."

TAKE NOTE—Horton Foote, who wrote this play, then the movie, also wrote *Tender Mercies*, another movie in this book.

TRIVIA QUIZ—What is the name of the old hymn with the phrase "come home" in the chorus which begins and ends the movie? (Answer No. 93)

> *If wrinkles must be written upon our brows, let them not be written on the heart. The spirit must not grow old.*
> —JAMES A. GARFIELD

Twelve Angry Men
Drama 1957

Director: Sidney Lumet

Starring: Henry Fonda, Lee J. Cobb, Ed Beagley, E. G. Marshall, Jack Klugman, Jack Warden, Martin Balsam, Edward Binns, John Fiedler, George Voskovec, Robert Webber, Joseph Sweeney

STORY CONCEPT—A young Spanish-American boy is tried for stabbing his father. Eleven on the jury vote guilty. One hesitates because he feels a death penalty verdict demands more deliberation. This dissenting vote causes the other jurors to reveal their priorities and prejudices.

THEME—The power to determine the future of another human being demands careful thought.

FAVORITE SCENE—During a discussion as to whether the key witness wore glasses or not, Mr. McCardle (Sweeney) observes that the witness, who wore no glasses on the stand, kept rubbing each side of his nose between his eyes. The jury agrees that this is something people do who wear glasses. However, the witness had retired for the night when he looked out the window and into an apartment where he saw the murder. No one wears glasses when they retire, therefore how could he have identified the murderer?

MEMORABLE LINES—An immigrant juror says: "One of the reasons this country is strong is because the jury system is not personal. Guilty or not guilty, it won't benefit us."

TAKE NOTE—All but three minutes of this film takes place in a jury room 16 x 24 feet.

TRIVIA QUIZ—How much per day was a juror paid at the time this movie was made in 1957? (Answer No. 94)

> *Right is right, even if everyone is against it, and wrong is wrong, even if everyone is for it.* —WILLIAM PENN

The Verdict

Drama 1982

Director: Sidney Lumet

Starring: Paul Newman, Jack Warden, Charlotte Rampling, James Mason, Milo O'Shea, Edward Binns

STORY CONCEPT—An alcoholic Boston lawyer who has sunk to the depths in his field has an opportunity to settle a medical malpractice case out of court. After seeing the defendant in a coma he decides to go to court and get not only justice but also bring the truth to light. It may be his last chance to redeem himself for all his wasted years.

THEME—Justice has the power to not only bless the downtrodden, but to rekindle the spirit of those who take up their cause.

FAVORITE SCENE—Frank Galvin (Newman) meets with the top lawyer of the defendants, Ed Concannon (Mason), and Judge Hogle (O'Shea) in his chambers. The judge asks Galvin how much it would take for him and his client to walk out of his office. Galvin replies that his client can't walk. The offer is $200,000, and Galvin rejects it. Judge Hogle pressures him by referring to his being disbarred, which Galvin denies. The trial date is set and the two walk out, leaving Galvin alone and muttering—dumb, dumb, dumb!

MEMORABLE LINES—Galvin looks at the lady in a coma for several minutes and then meets with the hospital administrator who wants to settle the case outside of court. Galvin: "If I take the money I'm lost—I'd just be a rich ambulance chaser!"

TAKE NOTE—Paul Newman is nominated for Best Actor award for the fifth time without winning. The sixth time is the charm in *The Color of Money* (1986).

TRIVIA QUIZ—How did Frank Galvin attempt to get business before he took this negligence case? (Answer No. 95)

A twinge of conscience is a glimpse of God. —PETER USTINOV

Vertigo
Thriller 1958

Director: Alfred Hitchcock

Starring: Jimmy Stewart, Kim Novak, Barbara Bel Geddes

STORY CONCEPT—A detective, forced to retire because of his fear of heights, is hired to shadow the wife of a former captain on the force. He saves her from drowning and falls in love with her. She is very confused and attempts suicide again, this time successfully. He has a nervous breakdown and is obsessed with the memory of her. One day he meets a stranger on the street who looks amazingly like her. He becomes acquainted with the stranger and proceeds to mold her in the image of his former love, which ends in tragic failure.

THEME—People who want to change others need to focus on the one they have the greatest influence over, themselves.

FAVORITE SCENE—Scottie Ferguson (Stewart) knocks at the door of a complete stranger (Novak) because she resembles his former love, Madelaine. Interestingly, she invites him in and his plan succeeds as she accepts his invitation to dinner.

MEMORABLE LINES—After saving Madelaine from drowning, Scottie says: "There's an old Chinese saying; once you've saved a person's life you're committed to care for them."

TAKE NOTE—The costume designer and Hitchcock worked together to give Madelaine's clothing an eerie appearance. Her trademark gray suit was chosen for its color because they thought it seemed odd for a blond woman to be wearing all gray. In 1982, 120 critics voted this movie number ten on the all-time International Critics' poll best movie list.

TRIVIA QUIZ—What does the word vertigo mean? (Answer No. 96)

Fear is the dark room where negatives are developed.
—ANONYMOUS

Witness
Drama/Romance 1985

Director: Peter Weir

Starring: Harrison Ford, Kelly McGillis, Lukas Haas,
Josef Sommer, Alexander Godunov, Danny Glover

• •

STORY CONCEPT—A city detective goes to great lengths by posing as an Amish to protect a young Amish boy, witness to a crime, when he finds his superiors are responsible for the murder.

THEME—People from two different worlds show their common humanity when they are willing to sacrifice their lives for each other.

FAVORITE SCENE—Rachel Lapp (McGillis) forgets her Amish upbringing and joins John Book (Ford) in dancing to a tune on the devil's instrument, the radio. They are interrupted by her grandfather Schaeffer (Sommer) who reprimands her and sends her to the house.

MEMORABLE LINES—Grandfather to young Samuel (Haas), who is handling a gun which belongs to the detective, John Book: "What you take into your hands, you take into your heart."

TAKE NOTE—Ford helps build the barn in the movie. He was a carpenter before he became an actor. Film was shot in Pennsylvania Amish country. The Amish house of Rachel has a mirror, but Amish houses do not have mirrors.

TRIVIA QUIZ—Why did no real Amish appear in this movie? (Answer No. 97)

If I trim myself to suit others I will soon whittle myself away.
—ANONYMOUS

When you get to wit's end, remember that God lives there.
—ANONYMOUS

Witness for the Prosecution
Drama 1957

Director: Billy Wilder

Starring: Charles Laughton, Elsa Lanchester, Marlene Dietrich, Tyrone Power, Una O'Conner

• •

STORY CONCEPT—A famous barrister, recovering from a near-fatal heart attack, is supposed to take it easy—but the challenge of a charmer, accused of murdering a rich widow, is too tempting. The charmer's only alibi is a calm and attractive wife who makes the barrister's task more difficult when she decides to be a witness for the prosecution and not the defense.

THEME—Words have the power to free or enslave.

FAVORITE SCENE—Sir Wilfrid Robarts (Laughton) returns to his home after a stay in the hospital. Nurse Plimsoll (Lanchester) has to watch him like a hawk. He evades her shots, pills, and mandates against cigars and brandy. But he never really fools her. It just makes him feel good to think that he does.

MEMORABLE LINES—Sir Wilfrid questions the housekeeper, Janet McKenzie (O'Conner), in court about the accused, Leonard Vole (Powers):

Robarts: I can understand why you're antagonistic toward him.
McKenzie: He's a scheming shiftless rascal! But I am not antagonistic toward him!

TAKE NOTE—This was Tyrone Powers' last film. He died suddenly at age 44 while filming *Solomon and Sheba* (1959). It was ironic because, when Tyrone was a young man, his father died in his arms after working the same night on a movie in Hollywood.

TRIVIA QUIZ—Where did Barrister Robarts attempt to hide his cigars? (Answer No. 98)

> *Being a woman is a terribly difficult trade, since it consists principally of dealing with men.* —JOSEPH CONRAD

Working Girl

Comedy/Romance 1988

Director: Mike Nichols

Starring: Melanie Griffith, Sigourney Weaver, Harrison Ford, Joan Cusack, Alex Baldwin

STORY CONCEPT—A hard-working young woman is stuck doing secretarial work until a lady executive takes her under her wing. The secretary shares some of her ideas with this new boss who shows confidence in her ability to take over while she goes on vacation. Then she learns her boss is going to use her ideas to cut a big deal, so she joins forces with another executive to make a deal of her own. The fur starts flying when she learns that her new partner, Jack (Ford), with whom she is falling in love, is also her boss' boyfriend.

THEME—A person's desire to get ahead may exceed the limits of propriety.

FAVORITE SCENE—Tess McGill (Griffith) tells Cyn (Cusack) of her big business ideas in her new position. Cyn tries to bring her back to reality by telling her about the song and dance she does in the privacy of her apartment—"but it doesn't mean I'm Madonna!"

MEMORABLE LINES—The morning after Tess passed out from drinking:

Tess: What did happen, exactly?
Jack: The earth moved. The angels wept. The Polaroids are, are, uh (gropes about in his coat pockets) are in my other coat. (Grins) Nothing happened! Nothing happened!

TAKE NOTE—Harrison Ford cut his chin in an auto accident when he was about twenty. In the movie, his character says that he was piercing his ear as a teen, and fainted and hit his chin on the toilet.

TRIVIA QUIZ—When Catherine Parker (Weaver) comes back to New York, what stuffed animal does she bring? (Answer No. 99)

If we choose to be no more than clods of clay, then we shall be used as clods of clay for braver feet to tread on. —MARIE CORELLI

Yankee Doodle Dandy

Biography 1942

Director: Michael Curtiz

Starring: James Cagney, Joan Leslie, Walter Huston,
Irene Manning, Jean Cagney

• •

STORY CONCEPT—The life and times of George M. Cohen, great composer, song writer, and entertainer told in flashback with Cohen going to the White House to see President Franklin D. Roosevelt, then retelling the story of his life.

THEME—Life's greatest joy comes from lifting up others.

FAVORITE SCENE—George's (Cagney) parents are retiring from show business and a surprise birthday party for his father (Huston) takes place. George's gift is a smoking jacket with a letter in the pocket. It is meant to be read in privacy but his father insists on reading it aloud. The heartfelt letter wishes God's blessings on his father and gives thanks for his parent's love. While reading the letter, George's father becomes so emotional he has to stop.

MEMORABLE LINES—George, on several different occasions after the family performance: "My mother thanks you. My father thanks you. My sister thanks you. And I thank you."

TAKE NOTE—William Cagney, James Cagney's brother, planted the seed in Mr. Cohen's mind for his brother to play this part because Jimmy had been branded by a few as being a communist sympathizer, and he felt this movie would display his true colors of patriotism. Cagney's sister in real life plays his sister, Jean, in the movie. For his patriotic songs, George M. Cohen was awarded the Congressional Medal of Honor by President Roosevelt.

TRIVIA QUIZ—What famous holiday is George Michael Cohen born on? (Answer No. 100)

> *When someone does something good, applaud! You will make two people happy.* —SAMUEL GOLDWYN

TRIVIA QUIZ Answers

1. "I'll Never Smile Again."
2. The African Queen.
3. Paper money.
4. His private life.
5. Irresistible impulse.
6. Ron Howard, the director.
7. He must not step on any cracks.
8. Ronald Reagan.
9. Four years (a regular tourist trap).
10. "Bang the Drum Slowly" (a song about a dying cowboy). They thought it would disturb dying Pearson.
11. "Heart And Soul" and "Chopsticks."
12. "Madness, madness!"
13. The Caine.
14. Ronald Reagan
15. Curley wouldn't tell him, but Mitch figured it out: to put his family before his job.
16. "Coal Miner's Daughter."
17. Hume Cronyn and Jessica Tandy.
18. Oprah Winfrey (Sofia).
19. Cool Runnings (Peace Be the Journey).
20. An old leather harness.
21. Dances with Wolves. He befriends a wolf who is following him to the Indian village. He gets off his horse to chase him away and the wolf thinks he is playing and jumps on him. Indians witness this and give him the name.
22. Ellen Mitchell (Weaver), the late president's wife.
23. Doberman.
24. A radio and a cake.
25. The unusual musical instrument she has strapped to her back as she walks away with her boyfriend. (The same instrument which Dr. Zhivago played.)

26. '49 Hudson.

27. Patti Page.

28. Not a thing. Cruise is bluffing.

29. In the minor leagues his shoes hurt him and he plays the rest of the game in his socks.

30. The Phoenix was a mythical bird that burns, then rises again from the ashes of its predecessors.

31. John F. Kennedy, Lyndon B. Johnson, Richard Nixon.

32. Frank Sinatra. (Won Best Supporting Actor award.)

33. He had one arm.

34. Weaving his own clothes.

35. He clicks when he talks.

36. The fifty officers who were executed after their recapture.

37. "He's not mean, he's just prejudiced!"

38. "I Got You Babe" by Sonny and Cher.

39. Tex Ritter, father of John Ritter.

40. Sorghum. (Try it on biscuits or toast.)

41. She wants him and his chorus to perform.

42. He is carrying Tibbs' suitcase.

43. Fear of water.

44. Judy Garland.

45. $4800 per year.

46. Catching flies with chopsticks.

47. Laverne of "Laverne and Shirley."

48. "It's Lucas! Suicide! He's gone out for the football team!"

49. John F. Kennedy.

50. Press her lips to her own hand.

51. Thumbing through the telephone book.

52. The cactus rose.

53. The late John Lennon.

54. "When the moon hits your eye, like a big-a pizza pie—that's amore!"

55. *Alice in Wonderland.*

56. 1928 Studebaker.

57. They are playing "76 Trombones," one of the marching songs.

58. GI Joe with a parachute.

59. Makes a cameo appearance.

60. Drinking champagne at the party in Sebastian's home.

61. He saw the Russian Sputnik in the October sky one night.

62. Caring for pigeons.

63. He asks about her golf game immediately after she had just told him.

64. Defend the children of the poor. Punish the evildoer.

65. He dresses as an angel and reads Peter's obituary with humor.

66. "Somewhere Over the Rainbow."

67. Newfoundland.

68. Twenty-One.

69. Death Penalty.

70. Judge Wapner (*The People's Court*) and *Jeopardy*.

71. Montgomery Clift.

72. He buys her a puppy.

73. *Rey and the High Himalayas* and *Bazaar* magazine.

74. Thirty.

75. Audrey Hepburn, Best Actress (in her first major role).

76. A gold ring (from their teeth).

77. Other nations and our own people would be alarmed and fearful.

78. His love for Joy Gresham.

79. Soda Pop.

80. Her picture hung in Andy's cell covering up a valuable secret.

81. Make 'Em Laugh.

82. Breyer's. (Wonder what that commercial cost?)

83. One year

84. Glenn Ford

85. Tess Harper

86. James Arness (Gunsmoke's Matt Dillon)

87. It begins to rain.

88. Robert Duvall.

89. Geena Davis.

90. "To Sir with Love."

91. He gives artificial respiration to a young lad whom they think has drowned but is in a coma.

92. A French coin.

93. "Softly and Tenderly," written by Will L. Thompson.

94. Three dollars a day.

95. He visits funeral homes and pretends to be a friend of the deceased, then hands out his business card. This is the reason he is called an "ambulance chaser."

96. Dizziness, a feeling that things are turning around.

97. Photography is not permitted by the Amish.

98. In his walking cane.

99. A gorilla.

100. The Fourth of July (really the third).

Actors Index

Directors Index

Genre Index

Fantasy

Musicals

Romance

Science Fiction

About the Author

Gynnath Ford has written four inspirational books. He has viewed thousands of movies over the past few decades. He is a motivational speaker who uses movies to inspire and encourage.

A Note to the Reader

Any information found in this book which is not accurate, please feel free to write to us and we will make corrections in future printings.

If you know the author of any of the quotations that do not have a source we are anxious to give credit where credit is due.

Perhaps you have a best liked movie. Send us the title and a couple of sentences as to why it's your favorite. We may include it in the next "Treasures of the Silver Screen" book from Highlands Publishing! Be sure to include your name so we can give you credit.

Quick Order Form

Fax orders: (615)-385-5915. Send this form.

Telephone orders: Call 1-800-331-5991 toll free.
Have your credit card ready.

Postal orders: Highlands Publishing, Box 50021, Nashville, TN 37205

I would like to order ———— copies of ***Treasures of the Silver Screen***
@ $14.99 each

(Non-profit groups and large orders please inquire about our discount pricing.)

Name: _____

Address: _____

City: _____ **State:** _____ **Zip:** _____

Telephone: _____

E-mail: _____

Sales tax: Please add 8.25% for books shipped to Tennessee addresses.

Shipping: Air—US: $4.00 for first book and $2.00 for each additional book. Surface—US: $2.00 for the first book and $2.00 for each additional book.

International: $9.00 for the first book and $5.00 for each additional book (estimate).

Payment: ❑ Check   ❑ Credit Card: ❑ Visa   ❑ Mastercard

Card number: _____ **Exp. date:** _____

Name on card: _____